THAILAND

John Hoskin

Photographs by Michael Freeman,
Luca Invernizzi Tettoni

D1513120

ODYSSEY GUIDES
Hong Kong

Grateful acknowlegement is made to the following authors and
publishers for permissions granted:

Hodder & Stoughton Ltd for
Teak-Wallah by Reginald Campbell, © Hodder & Stoughton 1935

Oxford University Press for
The Politician and Other Stories by Khamsing Srinawk
© Oxford University Press 1973

Distribution in the UK, Ireland, Europe and certain Commonwealth countries
by Hodder & Stoughton, Mill Road, Dunton Green, Sevenoaks, Kent TN13 2YA

Series Editor: Claire Banham
Contributing Editor: Avron Boretz
Picture Editor: Caroline Robertson
Maps, diagrams and artwork: Li Design Associates
Cover Concept: Raquel Jaramillo and Aubrey Tse

Photographs by Michael Freeman (5, 36–37, 44–45, 55, 58, 65, 72, 83, 91, 108–109,
136–137, 141, 144, 145, 152, 161, 172); Luca Invernizzi Tettoni (16, 20, 73, 80, 95,
100–101, 133, 156, 169, 173); Jacky Yip (50, 68); James Montgomery (10–11);
Helka Ahokas (3, 169); Ira Chaplin (97, 112); Ray Cranbourne (161); Nigel Hicks (121)

British Library Cataloguing in Publication Data has been applied for.

Produced by Twin Age Limited
Printed in Hong Kong

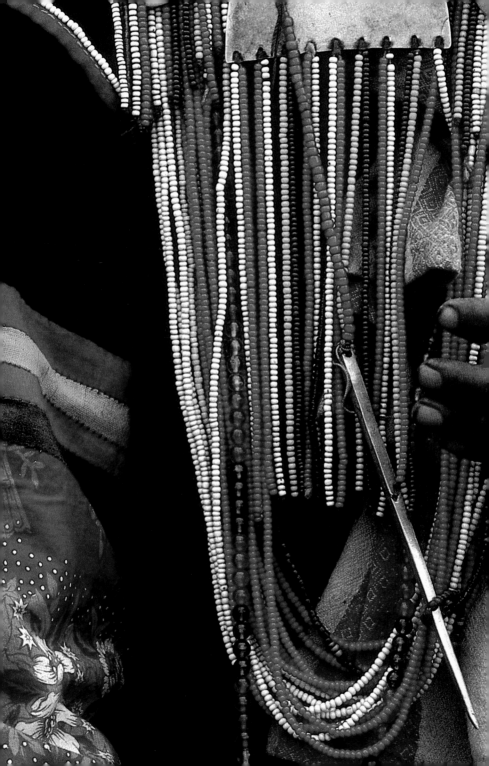

Contents

Map of Thailand

An Introduction to Thailand

Thailand has been called many things in its time: officially it was named Siam until 1939; popularly it has been dubbed the 'Land of Smiles'; and more recently the tourism authorities have adopted the promotional tag 'The Most Exotic Country in Asia'.

The capital, Bangkok, also has a varied nomenclature. 'Venice of the East' was a common sobriquet among foreign travellers in the days when it still had many *klongs* (canals). An equally outrageous comparison has been made with Paris in reference to the city's nightlife attractions. Most surprising, though, is that the name 'Bangkok' is not correct as far as the Thais are concerned. Bangkok means 'Village of the Wild Plum', which is what the original settlement was called before it became the capital. Once supreme status had been conferred, a more illustrious title was chosen. The first two words, Krung Thep or the City of Angels, suffice in daily use, although they are just the first of a whole mouthful which the *Guinness Book of World Records* lists as the longest place name. In Thai it reads: Krungthep Mahanakhon Bovorn Ratanakosin Mahintharayutthaya Mahadilokpop Noparatrat-chathani Burirom Udomratchaniveymahasathan Amornpiman Avatarnsathit Sakkathattiya-avisnukarmprasit. This translates as: Great City of Angels, the Supreme Repository of Divine Jewels, the Great Land Unconquerable, the Grand and Prominent Realm, the Royal and Delightful Capital City Full of Nine Noble Gems, the Highest Royal Dwelling and Grand Palace, the Divine Shelter and Living Place of the Reincarnated Spirits.

Rather than suggesting an identity problem, all this hints at a fascinating diversity in a rich and varied culture which, over the centuries, has benefited from a remarkably consistent development. Largely through the strength of the monarchy, Thailand has remained independent and, while absorbing some outside influences, has preserved its own distinct characteristics to an unusual degree.

In consequence, of all the sobriquets mentioned, that of 'most exotic country' rings true. The other names, of course, have some foundation. But the important point is that Thailand is different — different from its neighbours and different in the variety of attractions it offers.

The uniqueness of the place is frequently attributed to the fact that the nation was never colonized, as were all its neighbours without exception. Such a tradition of independence and the avoidance of European imperialism in the late 19th and early 20th centuries can, however, be regarded as much a symptom as a cause of such a dis-tinctive heritage. The Thais avoided imperial designs because of the

very traits — notably resilience and adaptability — that have always been theirs. The present sure sense of identity and way of life is thus the result of positive factors and not the mere absence of colonial imprints.

In a very real way, Thailand is an expression of its people, their sense of freedom coupled with a happy and contented disposition, their devotion to Buddhism, and their great respect for tradition. Inevitably, however, there has been change, much of it through the adaptation of foreign borrowings — at first from neighbours, later from the West — though Thailand remains exotic precisely because of the extent to which it has preserved its cultural integrity.

Nature has been generous with gifts as well. As varied as the historical and cultural sights are the natural scenes: idyllic tropical islands, unspoiled sandy beaches, jungle-clad mountains, rivers, caves, waterfalls, fertile plains supporting a patchwork of emerald green paddies.

Whether the preference is for lazing on a sun-drenched beach, trekking through jungles to visit remote hilltribe villages, or immersing yourself in local culture, there is truly something for all tastes.

Modernization and infrastructure development today bring the delights of Thailand within easy reach of the visitor, affording comfortable access to a host of pleasurable and rewarding experiences. Sightseeing, shopping, the thrilling nightlife, a wonderfully rich national cuisine, a kaleidoscope of places and scenes, all are part of this multi-faceted destination.

Domestic air travel, road and rail networks open up every part of the country to the visitor, while tourist facilities offer some of the world's finest hotels, adding a further dimension to the Thais' renowned tradition of gracious hospitality.

History

The Emergence of the Thais As a nation, the Thais were first united in the 13th century with the founding of the kingdom of Sukhothai. The history of the land now defined by the borders of Thailand, however, stretches back over a much longer period, and is characterized by a succession of states and civilizations and the mingling of diverse peoples, before the Thais finally became dominant.

Occupying the central and western part of the Indochinese peninsula, the region was originally settled by groups of non-Mongoloid peoples (perhaps the ancestors of the Malaysian and Philippine Negritos, or of the Polynesians). Recent excavations at Ban Chiang in northeast Thailand indicate an advanced culture flourishing in the area as far back as 3600 BC. These original inhabitants were subsequently subject to diverse waves of immigration from the north, as well as various outside cultural influences, and they gave way gradually to the Thais, who then became the principal heirs to the region's cultural development.

The Impact of India The first important shaping force on what was to become Thailand, indeed on the whole of Southeast Asia, was the impact of Indian civilization. This was to provide the basic mould for the region's culture, its artistic endeavours and its social and religious patterns.

In the second and third centuries, Indian traders sailed during the winter across the Bay of Bengal to the Malay peninsula or through the Straits of Malacca. At ports along these shores they would lay up until the prevailing winds changed with the arrival of the summer monsoon, which enabled them to continue their voyage to points south and east. Gradually, in the course of this contact, India came to leave an indelible stamp on the whole of Southeast Asia.

The process of Indianization was long and slow and probably effected in various ways. The seaborne merchants themselves were unlikely to have had much impact on indigenous cultures, but Indian princes could have set themselves up to rule over local communities, subsequently intermarrying so as to legitimize their assumption of authority. Alternatively, local rulers could have invited Indian brahmans and scholars to serve as administrators, advisers and astrologers at their courts. Brahmanism, the ancient form of Hinduism, had a special attraction in that it lent support to the idea of a god-king, a concept most spectacularly embraced by the Khmer of Angkor.

India was the cradle of Buddhism as well, and this religion was also implanted in the region. While the Thais eventually adopted Theravada Buddhism, strains of Brahmanism persisted and even today it is Brahman priests who conduct the major royal rites and ceremonies.

Dvaravati From such a cultural base a number of independent civilizations grew up in Indochina, and three in particular were to have a profound and lasting effect on the Thais. The first of these was Dvaravati, a vaguely united collection of city states with, most likely, a power base at what is now the Thai town of Nakhon Pathom, west of Bangkok. With a population of probably Mon origin, the kingdom flourished in the Chao Phraya River basin from the sixth or seventh to the 11th century. The people of Dvaravati were Theravada Buddhists and it is probable that the Thais (originally animists) were first converted to this faith through contact with the Mon. Besides religion, Dvaravati also strongly influenced sculpture and temple architecture.

The latter is witnessed to good effect in the *chedis* at Lamphun, the former capital of an offshoot Mon kingdom known as Haripunchai.

The Kingdom of Srivijaya Roughly contemporary with Dvaravati and affecting the early development of southern Thailand was the kingdom of Srivijaya. This civilization dominated the Malay peninsula and Indonesian archipelago from the eighth to near the end of the 13th century. It also clearly moulded the culture of southern Thailand and a good deal of distinct sculpture has been discovered at Chaiya and surrounding districts near the modern town of Surat Thani.

The Khmer By the 11th century a new force held sway in the eastern and central parts of what is now Thailand. The Khmer, whose great civilization centred on Angkor, gave rise to an empire which at its height spread a cultural and artistic heritage to which the Thais would later become heirs. The Khmer influence was especially felt at such provincial centres as Lopburi, which gives its name to the distinctive sculpture of the period, and at Phimai where the finest examples of Khmer religious architecture to be seen outside Kampuchea are found.

Nan Chao It is certain that a predominantly Thai state, Nan Chao, existed between the seventh and 13th centuries, located in what are now parts of the southwestern Chinese provinces of Yunnan and Sichuan.

When Nan Chao fell to the Mongols in 1253 there was likely a mass migration of Thais to the south, but this almost certainly only boosted a Thai population that had been gradually settling in the region for centuries.

Throughout this time the Thais were becoming more numerous and more organized. Basically an agrarian people, they began to establish small city states or clusters of villages ruled over by one chieftain.

The Sukhothai Kingdom The dawn of the 13th century heralded a new era in the region. The power of the Khmer was now well in decline, while the Thais were becoming stronger. Eventually, by uniting their forces, two Thai chieftains, Phor Khun Pha Muang and Phor Khun Bang Klang Thao, defeated the forward defenders of the Khmer empire and founded the first Thai capital at Sukhothai in about 1238; the name appropriately translates as 'Dawn of Happiness'.

Phor Khun Bang Klang Thao was proclaimed king, taking the title Sri Intratit and establishing the first Thai dynasty, Phra Ruang. As a fully independent kingdom, Sukhothai lasted little more than 100 years, but in that time it laid the essential foundations of the Thai nation.

Sukhothai represents the first unification of the Thai people under a single monarch and a cohesive national religion, Theravada Buddhism.

It also witnessed the first flowering of distinct Thai styles of art and architecture, and the political, social, cultural and artistic roots of the modern nation can all, to a greater or lesser degree, be traced back to the Sukhothai Kingdom.

Sukhothai's golden age came in the third reign, that of King Ramkamhaeng the Great (1279–98). Under his masterful leadership the kingdom was consolidated through considerable territorial gains and the codification of social and administrative principles. It was Ramkamhaeng who created the Thai alphabet and left a lasting document to his achievements in his famous stone inscription, now housed at the National Museum in Bangkok.

Paralleling internal developments at this time was the vital external contact with Sri Lanka, the world centre for Theravada Buddhism. By the mid-12th century, Thai, Mon and Khmer monks had begun to journey to Sri Lanka. On their return to their homeland, some Thai monks started to preach Buddhism according to the Sri Lankan school in the southern town of Nakhon Si Thammarat. It was here that Ramkamhaeng, on a tour of his territories, first came into contact with the revitalized form of Theravada Buddhism. Embracing the religion whole-heartedly, he installed monks of the Singhalese school at his capital, and their influence was later strengthened when missions made direct contact with Sri Lanka.

The impact of all this cannot be underestimated. The art and architecture of Sukhothai is characterized by many Sri Lankan forms in, for example, decorative stucco work, line engraving and, most visibly, in the adoption of the bell-shaped *chedi*.

Sukhothai sculpture, arguably the finest artistic achievement of the period, also owes a great debt to Sri Lankan influences which are apparent in the Buddha's supernatural physical features — cranial protuberance, extended earlobes, arms long enough to reach the knees and flat-soled feet with projecting heels — all of which follow descriptions of the Enlightened One in the Pali texts.

None of Sukhothai's other eight reigns can rival that of King Ramkamhaeng in terms of military, social, religious and cultural achievement. Yet the kingdom's strength was not yet expended. The fourth monarch, Loe Thai (1299–1346), is notable for his construction of the third major city, Jakungrao, later known as Kamphaengphet, about 80 kilometres (50 miles) southwest of Sukhothai.

Ayutthaya As a sovereign state, Sukhothai was in decline by the late 14th century. During the reign of King Maha Tammaraja II (1368–c1399) it became a vassal of Ayutthaya, a young, dynamic Thai kingdom that had swiftly risen to power in the Chao Phraya River basin to the south.

Sukhothai was finally eclipsed by Ayutthaya in 1438. Vestiges of its former glory lingered on until the 16th century when the city was abandoned. Si Satchanalai suffered the same fate and, of the first Thai kingdom's three principal sites, only Kamphaengphet survived as a living settlement.

Ayutthaya was to be the heart of the Thai state for the next 350 years. It was not, however, the only kingdom of Thais. A northern state, centred on Chiang Mai and known as Lanna, managed to maintain independence long after Sukhothai had been eclipsed.

Lanna was founded in the latter part of the 13th century and was a close ally of Sukhothai. Its first king, Mengrai, was a Thai-Lao prince whose father had ruled a small kingdom based at Chiang Saen where the northern Thais first came to unite. Historically the northerners maintained a separate development, and while Lanna did not always sustain centralized control, northern Thailand survived as a collection of quasi-independent states until the early 20th century.

On succeeding his father, Mengrai gathered several small tribes together and quickly set about enlarging his domain. He founded successive capitals at Chiang Rai and Fang before eventually consolidating his power with the creation of Chiang Mai in 1296 as the centre of his newly-won kingdom. Domination of the northern region was completed when he defeated the Mon kingdom of Haripunchai (modern-day Lamphun) in 1281.

King Mengrai died in 1317, reputedly struck by lightning, but he had successfully established a dynasty and made Lanna a sovereign entity. But with the decline of its southern ally, Sukhothai, security was never assured and Ayutthaya was always to be a thorn in its side. Lanna did, nevertheless, blossom in the 15th century during the reign of King Tilokaraja (1442–87), who succeeded in holding sway over most of the area that is now northern Thailand.

By the 16th century Lanna was weakening, partly due to internal rifts and partly because of virtually continuous hostilities with Ayutthaya (a major defeat was suffered at Lampang in 1515). And then there was a new menace in the shape of the Burmese, who came to threaten the whole of Thailand and managed to overpower Lanna in 1556. For the next two centuries the north was, in one form or another, subject to Burma. When King Taksin of Thonburi finally expelled the Burmese from Thai territory in the late 1770s, Lanna was merely a collection of semi-independent princely states, though Chiang Mai remained the most important. This state of affairs remained until the 1930s when the north was brought fully under the control of the central Thai government in Bangkok.

The separate history of Lanna is still evidenced today by the characteristic art and architecture of the area and the somewhat distinctive traits of the northerners — more easy-going and more fun-loving than their southern counterparts. However, mainstream history of Thailand belongs to Ayutthaya.

The city of Ayutthaya, on the Chao Phraya river 85 kilometres (53 miles) north of Bangkok, was founded in 1350 by King U Thong (later crowned Ramathibodi). Situated at the junction of the Pa Sak and Lopburi Rivers with the Chao Phraya, it needed just the cutting of a canal to turn it into an easily defended island, and its network of communication canals set the pattern of riverine settlement that has been followed ever since by Thai communities.

Ayutthaya quickly came to take over the role of religious, cultural and commercial capital of the Thais and was later to be the model for Bangkok. At the height of its power in the 17th century, Ayutthaya, exercising control over nearly all of Thailand except the north, was one of the biggest and most magnificent cities in the Orient. It is claimed to have had a population of one million. The city walls enclosed glorious palaces, hundreds of temples, and separate quarters for the military, scholars, artists, artisans and so forth. Internal communication was via an extensive network of waterways and roads. Outside the walls were the settlements, or factories as they were known, of various foreign communities, European as well as Asian.

From the conquest of Sukhothai and the containment of Lanna, Ayutthaya went from strength to strength and, in addition to what is now Thai territory, also ruled over parts of Laos and Kampuchea (Angkor, a shadow of its former self, was defeated by the Thais in 1431). It was not unchallenged, though, and Burma was a constantly threatening presence to the west. Steady, if periodic, warfare was conducted against the Burmese.

The full flowering of Ayutthaya's glory, its cultural achievements and its wealth, came in the 17th century and was based on trade. The Thais themselves were not great merchants — the lower classes were agriculturists, the nobles were administrators — but they permitted others to carry on trade under a royal monopoly. With China and Japan effectively closed to outsiders, Ayutthaya became a major entrepôt for the expanding East-West trade. First, in 1511, came the Portuguese, then the Dutch in 1605, the English in 1612, and the Danes in 1621. The French, eventually to have great, albeit ill-fated, influence at Court, arrived in 1662.

As a centre of international interest, Ayutthaya came into its own during the reign of King Narai (1656—88). King Louis XIV of France sent two embassies to the Court of King Narai in attempts to win favour over his European competitors, notably the English and the

Dutch. Thus came about one of the most curious moments in Thailand's history.

Since the mid-16th century Ayutthaya had followed a course of internationalism that allowed certain foreigners with special skills to be taken into the king's employ. Accordingly, there arose an age of European adventurers, cunning, greedy, colourful characters who, like the Englishman Samuel White, ostensibly served King Narai although their main concern was to amass fortunes for themselves. Of them all, none rose so high as the remarkable Constantine Phaulkon (the Falcon), a British seaman of Greek origin who first established himself as a trader at Ayutthaya, then subsequently achieved a meteoric rise in the king's service. As Narai's chief minister, he became the second most important man in the land. Never before nor ever again did a foreigner hold such a dominant position in Thailand.

Phaulkon served at the Court of Ayutthaya for only eight years, exercising supreme influence for less than half that period, yet in his time he became a legend. He was a man of undisputed talents and, by his own accounts, was dedicated to serving his adopted king and country. The Thai courtiers thought otherwise.

The Greek's downfall was brought about by his favouring the French embassies. This was largely done in good faith — at least it can be argued so — but besides trade concessions, the French were seeking to convert King Narai to Catholicism. Fearing a Gallic takeover, a band of courtiers led what has become known as the Revolution of 1688. Phaulkon was executed for treason, the French were unceremoniously kicked out and King Narai, with fortunate timing, died of natural causes.

The dynastic change thus brought about effectively closed Thailand to official foreign relations for the next one-and-a-half centuries. The nation once again became introspective and was weakened by internal squabbles. In 1767 the Burmese made an all-out attack, captured Ayutthaya, systematically looted it, killed or took into slavery all but 10,000 inhabitants and razed the city. It was the end of an era.

Ferocious though the Burmese attack was, the invaders were unable to consolidate any territorial gains. The Thais, showing their characteristic resilience, were quickly rallied under General Taksin, who had set up a resistance base at Thonburi on the opposite bank of the Chao Phraya from Bangkok. Before the close of the year that had witnessed the wholesale destruction of Ayutthaya, he had established a new capital, had been crowned king and had begun to reunite the people. He succeeded in a masterful counter attack and within a couple of years had rid the country of the Burmese presence.

Thonburi was to remain the new Thai capital for 15 years although

Taksin, apparently a better military tactician than monarch, showed increasing signs of megalomania and, by 1782, had completely alienated himself from the people. The army commander, General Chakri, was recalled from an expedition in Laos to settle the matter.

Taksin was by now incurably insane and Chakri had no alternative but to order his execution, which was carried out in the manner then prescribed for royalty — being placed in a velvet sack and beaten over the head with a sandalwood club so that no blood was shed. Chakri was then popularly acclaimed king and was crowned Rama I, thus becoming the founder of the present Chakri Dynasty.

The Chakri Dynasty The year 1782 was a momentous one, for not only was a new dynasty created but the nation was also to receive a new capital. Chakri had decided to move his power base across the Chao Phraya to Bangkok for strategic purposes.

Bangkok at that time comprised little more than a customs post and a huddle of huts belonging to Chinese traders but, being on the east bank of the river, it was a more easily defended site than Thonburi should the Burmese ever try to move in again from the west. Defence was not Rama I's only purpose in looking for a new capital; he also desired to wipe out the memory of defeat and restore national pride with the construction of a city that would recreate the lost glory of Ayutthaya.

Accordingly, the first reign witnessed enormous activity as Bangkok was rapidly transformed from a sleepy riverside village into a metropolis that replicated Ayutthaya as faithfully as possible. Building was carried out at a rapid pace and by 1785, Wat Phra Keo (Temple of the Emerald Buddha), the royal chapel in the grounds of the Grand Palace, had been completed. Here was enshrined the image of the Emerald Buddha which Rama I, when he was Taksin's general, had brought back from Laos and the fate of which is closely linked to that of the nation in popular belief.

King Rama I died in 1809. In the succeeding two reigns Bangkok was further expanded and embellished until it was one of the most magnificent cities in the Orient, a worthy successor to Ayutthaya.

King Mongkut Throughout the early years of the new dynasty everything had followed as closely as possible the model of Ayutthaya, but with the fourth reign, that of King Mongkut (1851−68), there was to be a radical shift in emphasis. The nation's introspective stance was abandoned and Thailand began again to look towards the outside world, especially the West, for ways in which to modernize.

King Mongkut was possessed of an intelligent and inquiring mind, and during the 27 years he had spent in the monkhood before ascending the throne he had proved himself a scholar of considerable

How Buddhism Emerged in Thailand

Buddha means 'The Enlightened One' and is the title of a prince named Siddhartha Gautama, born in around 500 BC in northern India, who renounced his life of luxury to spend long years wandering as an ascetic. At last, fasting and meditating under a tree, he attained enlightenment.

From then until his death he expounded his insight into ultimate reality; his teachings encouraged people to take full responsibility for their thoughts and actions on a path to spiritual growth.

Buddha's followers formed communities of monks and nuns, where they lived disciplined lives and sought wisdom. For 500 years, while Buddhism spread throughout India, all the teaching was oral. In the third century BC this early form of Buddhism, called Hinayana (Theravada in Thailand) or the 'Lesser Vehicle', took root permanently in Sri Lanka and spread outwards into other parts of South and Southeast Asia.

In India a new form of Buddhism appeared, called Mahayana or the 'Greater Vehicle', which had a more popular appeal. Though sharing basic doctrines with Hinayana, its emphasis changed. Compassion was its chief virtue and its ideal was the Bodhisattva, a perfected individual who gave up heavenly bliss (*nirvana*) in order to return to earth and help others.

Buddha was not treated like one god. Countless 'mythical Buddhas' were invented to embody all of his aspects and their images were worshipped in temples. By the first century, scriptures (sutras) laid down doctrines and monastic rules, and recorded Buddha's sermons as they were remembered. Mahayana Buddhism spread to China, central Asia, Japan and other parts of east Asia, as well as Vietnam and Angkorian Cambodia.

The religion first came to Thailand before the division of the two basic Buddhist sects, in the seventh century. It was then, according to tradition, that the Indian emperor Ashoka sent two missionaries to the 'Land of Gold'. This has been tentatively identified as the Mon kingdom of Dvaravati centred on the town of Nakhon Pathom, west of present-day Bangkok.

The country of this time was not yet dominated by the Thais, though those who had begun to migrate from southern China would have received their first contact with Buddhism through mingling with the Mon.

While the seeds of the religion were sown early and had come directly from India, the form of Buddhism that was eventually adopted by the Thais was developed later from the Sri Lankan school.

By the time of the founding of the first Thai sovereign state at Sukhothai in the early 13th century, Buddhist monks in the southern part of the country had made contact with Sri Lanka and with its doctrine of Hinayana or Theravada Buddhism based on Pali texts.

Sukhothai's greatest monarch, King Ramkamhaeng (reigned 1279–98), reputedly met with these southern monks and invited them back to his capital to establish Buddhism according to the Sri Lanka school. Theravada Buddhism was embraced by the Thai nation and thrived to become one of the most vital, cohesive forces in Thai society.

After Sukhothai was eclipsed by the Ayutthaya kingdom, Theravada Buddhism continued to flourish. It enjoyed the support of the monarchy, which was responsible for the building of countless temples and monasteries to sustain both the communities of monks and the spiritual needs of the lay people.

With the fall of Ayutthaya to the Burmese in 1767, many of the nation's religious books were lost in the destruction of the former capital. Buddhism flourished again in the Ratanakosin (Bangkok) period, notably receiving renewed impetus during the reign of King Mongkut, Rama IV (1851–68), who was himself a monk for 27 years prior to ascending to the throne. In an effort to purify religious practice he created a second, stricter monastic sect, Thammayut, which still coexists with the traditional Mahanikai order.

Today, Theravada Buddhism in Thailand is as strong as ever, professed and practised by over 95 percent of the population. It is a religion both vital and visible in daily life.

The Spread of Buddhism

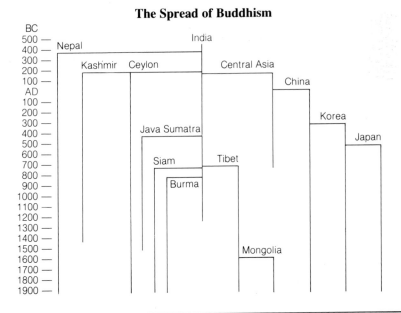

attainment in languages, history and astronomy. Unfortunately he is known to the West, if at all, as the king of *The King and I*, a musical production based on the reminiscences of Anna Leonowens, one-time governess to his children. What she wrote and the musical her books inspired were, however, so rife with cultural and historical inaccuracies that the film *The King and I* has always been banned in Thailand.

Rather than the archetypal Oriental despot Ms Leonowens chose to portray, King Mongkut was a most enlightened monarch and it was he who set the nation on the path to modernization and put it on the international map. Not since the ill-fated French embassies of the late 17th century had Thailand made overtures to the outside world, nor encouraged foreign interests. All that changed in 1855 when King Mongkut signed a mutually favourable trade agreement with Sir John Bowring, envoy of Queen Victoria. In so doing he opened up the way for Thailand's modern development while, at the same time, cleverly side-stepping any colonial designs of the Western powers.

The British treaty was followed in quick succession by similar accords with other major European powers and with the United States. International trade now began to flourish and Thailand rapidly adapted itself to providing the necessary infrastructure for commercial activity. Communication networks were expanded (Bangkok got its first proper roads in the 1860s) and public services and utilities were developed along Western lines.

The build-up of foreign trade not only brought Westerners flocking to the country, it also gave a new role to Chinese immigrants who for centuries had made up a sizeable minority in the major cities. The Thai Chinese had for long engaged in commerce, but now the number of positions for clerks, wholesalers and the whole army of middlemen who keep the wheels of trade turning mushroomed like never before. The Chinese were not slow to take advantage of the new situation.

Immigration today is strictly controlled and the Chinese who have settled in Thailand over the centuries have been almost completely assimilated. Today, it is difficult for the visitor to tell the difference between someone of pure Thai stock and a person of Chinese origin. Nevertheless, the commercial prosperity of Thailand has been brought about largely through the energy and business acumen of the overseas Chinese.

Mongkut's son and successor, King Chulalongkorn, Rama V (reigned 1868–1910), continued and greatly expanded the policies of his father. He transformed the machinery of state, following the main Western models, and successfully introduced sweeping reforms (including the abolition of slavery), reorganized government ministries and broadly adapted foreign concepts of administration, justice, education and public welfare.

In the succeeding reign of King Vajiravudh (1910–25) further reforms — such as the establishment of compulsory education — were introduced. On the international scene, Vajiravudh brought Thailand into World War I on the side of the Allies.

Political Changes With so much modernization taking place, it was almost inevitable that the political system would change. For centuries Thai kings had had absolute power; they were literally 'Lords of Life'. But by the 1920s Vajiravudh's successor, King Prajadhipok (reigned 1925–35), was considering ways to liberalize the system. Events, however, overtook ideas, and the bloodless revolution of 1932 changed the system of government to a constitutional monarchy. Prajadhipok accepted the situation but must have felt uneasy with its development and abdicated in 1935, living in self-imposed exile in England until his death in 1941. He was succeeded by King Ananda, his nephew, who was killed in the palace under mysterious circumstances in 1946. Ananda's brother, the present King Bhumibol Adulyadej, Rama IX, then ascended the throne.

Since the revolution of 1932, Thailand has had 22 prime ministers and the Constitution has been changed a number of times. The role of the military has remained strong and some 16 coups, successful and abortive, have to varying degrees disturbed the peaceful evolution of government though not socio-economic development in any fundamental way. The role of the monarchy, albeit limited by the Constitution, continues to have a powerful stabilizing effect and the people's respect and love for the king is probably as great as it ever was.

During World War II, Thailand was occupied by the Japanese and the then-government of Field Marshal Phibul complied with the occupiers. However, this was largely an acceptance of a de facto situation and the Thai minister in Washington refused to deliver his government's declaration of war on the United States and instead set about organizing a Free Thai movement in co-operation with the American Office of Strategic Services (OSS).

In the postwar years the nation has moved slowly and with difficulty towards establishing an effective democracy. In 1973 a bloody student uprising succeeded in ousting the repressive regime of military officers Thanom Kittikachorn and Praphas Charusathien, but was followed by a violent backlash three years later when right- and left-wing students clashed at Thammasat University in Bangkok.

More recently, despite the continued occurrence of coups every few years and the on-going strength of the military, Thailand is gradually

Everyday Religious Objects

Amulets (Phra Phum) — Thais have great faith in the power and efficacy of amulets and most will wear at least one (some have half a dozen or more) on a neck chain. Commonly contained in a gold case with a clear plastic front, these amulets are usually tiny Buddha images which have been blessed, though less commonly they can be likenesses of famous monks. Some charms are considered to bring general good fortune and well-being, while others are held to have specific powers such as offering protection from bullets or knives.

Spirit Houses (Phra Phi) — In the garden or compound of virtually every house, office and public building there is a spirit house. Usually raised on a short column, these miniature dwellings, in the form of little temples or old Thai-style houses, are provided as homes for the spirits who inhabit that particular plot of land. The belief is that while humans have taken over use of the site, the spirits must still have their own dwelling so that they do not become angered and thus bring misfortune. Much ceremony surrounds the positioning of a spirit house and once erected it must be constantly cared for with food offerings and garlands so that the spirits remain contented.

Puang-Ma-Lai — This is a small fragrant garland made of jasmine, the loop usually decorated with an orchid tassel. It is used as a kind of general purpose offering, and is placed over Buddha images, on spirit houses and so forth.

Sai Sin — Worn like a bracelet, the *sai sin* is a thin piece of cotton cord which has been blessed by a monk and is believed to give protection against evil spirits. A *sai sin* is also placed by monks around the interior of a house or office during the ceremony to bless a new building.

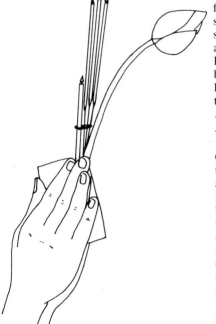

Temple Offerings — When praying at the temple Thais place three objects of offering in front of the Buddha image — a candle, a lotus flower and incense. The candle symbolizes the light of understanding, and the lotus is considered an exalted flower, special to the Buddha. For the incense there must be three sticks which represent the Buddhist Triple Gem, standing for the Buddha, his teachings (the *dhamma*), and the monkhood (the *sangha*).

Gold Leaf — Sold in little booklets, tiny squares of wafer-thin gold leaf are traditionally pressed on to Buddha images. In part this is done because Thais feel it is appropriate that the image is thus richly adorned, though they also believe that the practice will bring them certain benefits. There are three especially important places to put the gold leaf: on the mouth so that the giver will be blessed with good speech or sweet talk; on the head so as to become more wise; and on the chest to ensure a good heart in the sense of both health and kindness.

evolving its own characteristic style of democracy and can be numbered among the most stable countries in Southeast Asia. Also, regardless of the ups and downs of political administration, Thailand's economic development has been consistent and rapid and, taking into consideration all factors, the nation is well poised to sustain growth.

Geography

A tropical country lying approximately between latitudes 6° and 21° north, Thailand is located almost equidistant between India and China. Bordered by Burma on the west, Laos in the north, Kampuchea in the east and Malaysia in the south, it covers an area of 514,000 square kilometres (198,475 square miles) — about the size of, for example, France — and extends 1,650 kilometres (1,025 miles) on a north-south line and 800 kilometres (500 miles) east to west. The country's outline is extremely irregular, frequently likened to an elephant's head and trunk, and so practical distances are much less than maximum limits.

Thailand is divided into four topographical regions: the fertile Central Plain traversed north-south by the Chao Phraya River and its tributaries; the mountainous North where the country's highest peak, Doi Inthanon, rises to 2,565 metres (8,415 feet) (thus all mountains are well below the tree-line and are typically forest-clad); the semi-arid plateau of the Northeast; and the narrow isthmus of the South, typified by hilly rainforests and a coastline indented by coves and bays with some superb beaches and numerous offshore islands.

Thailand is an extremely fertile land, as well as being well endowed with various natural resources; major export items include rice, maize, tin, rubber, tapioca products and textiles. The Gulf of Thailand is also rich in marine life.

Lush vegetation abounds and there are many species of trees, shrubs and flowers, perhaps most notable among the latter being the nearly 1,000 different varieties of orchids. Fauna include elephants, tigers, leopards, snakes, monkeys and hundreds of species of birds and butterflies. Sadly, as in many other places, the numbers of the larger wild animals—elephants and tigers in particular—have declined drastically in recent decades.

People

Thailand's population stands at 55 million (1989 estimate). The majority of the people are ethnically Thai, though there is considerable ethnic diversity. Chinese, Mon, Khmer, Burmese, Malay, Lao, Persian and Indian strains are, to varying degrees, mixed with Thai stock. Ethnic minorities — chiefly northern hilltribes, Lao, Vietnamese and

Kampuchean refugees, as well as a number of South Asian Indian and other permanent foreign residents — account for about six percent of the total population.

Consequently there is a noticeable variation in physiognomy and physique among Thais, not just regionally but also locally. In one small village, for example, it is possible to see a wide range of skin tones. Taking districts as a whole, the inhabitants of the North display more Lao and Burmese traits; the South is influenced by Malays; and in Bangkok roughly half the population has some Chinese blood.

Thailand remains basically an agrarian society and about three-quarters of the population are connected with agriculture in some form or another. Virtually all major commercial, financial and industrial activity is concentrated in Bangkok, where more than one-tenth of the population resides. Moves towards decentralization—the much-heralded Eastern Seaboard Development, for example — are being made but for the time being the capital bears the greatest burden in sustaining national progress.

Consequently there is a marked difference between Bangkok and upcountry areas, and even the second city, Chiang Mai, is less than one-fortieth the size of Greater Bangkok. Provincial towns are growing — Khon Kaen in the Northeast, for instance, has expanded rapidly in the last few years — but travel around Thailand still presents a mostly rural picture with scenes of a way of life that continues to follow an age-old annual cycle dictated by the agricultural year and punctuated by numerous festivals both religious and secular.

The Thai Lifestyle

In character the Thais are an easy-going, hospitable and fun-loving people; they also have a strong pride and sense of national identity that springs from a long adherence to tradition.

The visitor arriving in Bangkok is unwittingly confronted with a paradox. The capital appears as a modern, Western-style metropolis. Nevertheless, at the same time it is typically and indelibly Thai. Similarly there appears to be a great disparity between lifestyles in Bangkok and those upcountry. Certainly the capital has a burgeoning middle class and its members, particularly the young, seem won over by mostly Western cultural styles. The impact of alien values cannot be denied yet they have not, either in Bangkok or in the rural districts, displaced home-grown ways and attitudes — Thais are Thais, and whether some might prefer McDonald's to a street noodle stall has little effect on underlying values.

Among the more prosaic traditions affecting lifestyle are the deep

Mythological Figures

Thai culture, drawing on various sources in the process of evolving from a melting pot of peoples and beliefs, is rich in legends and myths. Inhabiting these tales is a large cast of heroes, demons, giants and mythical creatures often half-human and half-animal. The more important figures are portrayed in statuary and decorative work and among those commonly seen in temple compounds and elsewhere are:

Garuda — Usually depicted as having the head and legs of a bird, the torso of a man and winged arms, the *garuda* is the king of birds and the traditional mount of the god Vishnu. It is half-brother of the *naga*, its sworn enemy and with whom it is often engaged in epic struggle. As a powerful and divine carrier, the *garuda* has come to be used as an official symbol in matters relating to the Thai king and, for example, it appears at the head of state documents and official letters.

Naga — An offspring of the same father as the *garuda* but having a different mother, the *naga* is the mythical king of serpents. It is also a water symbol. Often a multi-headed creature, one Buddhist legend describes a seven-headed *naga* which spread its cobra-like hoods to shelter the meditating Buddha; this is commonly depicted in statues of the Lopburi period. In architecture, balustrades in the form of a *naga* frequently flank the stairs leading up to a temple, as at Doi Suthep in Chiang Mai.

Apsara — One of a number of beautiful celestial nymphs which appeared from the mythical Sea of Milk as it was churned by the gods. Their destiny is to dance and fulfil the desires of the gods. In Thai temple mural paintings, *apsaras* are often shown floating in the skies.

Kinnari — A mythical being with the head and torso of a woman and the wings and legs of a bird which inhabits the legendary Himalayan forests. There is a male counterpart known as *kinnara*.

Yaksha — Any one of a race of giants having cruel faces with long, pointed teeth. Their roles vary in different myths and they can be either forces of evil or supernatural attendants of the gods. In statuary they are most often seen as guardians, standing with their backs to a temple to prevent the entry of devils.

Hanuman — The monkey warrior who leads an army against the evil Totsakan to rescue Sita, the wife of Prince Rama, in the story of the *Ramakien*. He is a magical, mischievous creature, always up to tricks and hence one of the most popular and best-known characters in the *Ramakien*.

respect held for elders and teachers, a well-developed sense of propriety and a pride in personal appearance and seemly conduct.

When it comes down to the effect of lifestyle on the visitor, the Thais' most essential trait is that of being a fun-loving people. Life is to be enjoyed and this is well illustrated by oft-used Thai words like *sanuk*, to have fun, *sabai*, meaning well in the sense of feeling good, or that stock response to the question 'Where are you going', *pai teeo*, which roughly translates as 'Just going for a stroll, seeing whatever is to be seen'.

This well-developed sense of fun finds expression in myriad ways, from the numerous festivals that dot the national calendar to sports both modern, such as football, and traditional, such as kickboxing or kite-flying. But most of all it is witnessed most wonderfully in food. Thais are not big eaters but they are great eaters, taking delight in little snacks several times throughout the day. It is thus not surprising that they have developed one of the world's great cuisines.

Beliefs

One highly visible indication that traditional beliefs continue to play an important role in daily life is the ubiquitous spirit house (see page 26). Other shrines — the most famous in Bangkok being that to the Hindu deity Brahma at the old site of the Erawan Hotel—are also commonly seen. They are widely held to have powers to grant wishes and are visited daily by hundreds of supplicants seeking all kinds of good fortune, from the desire for motherhood to winning the lottery. It is a reciprocal business and once a wish has been answered the supplicant will return to the shrine to make an offering of thanks—often lavishly prepared food or simply flowers and incense.

Amulets worn on chains around the neck are also popular — you will sometimes see a man sporting a dozen or more (see page 27). While not all Thais have the same faith in amulets, most certainly have a great belief in astrologers and other kinds of fortune tellers and will not embark on any major undertaking without first consulting about the most auspicious time. Ceremonies with monks and sometimes Brahman priests (as with the laying of foundation stones) are also held essential to bless the opening of new buildings, new companies or even the arrival of a new aircraft for Thai International.

The widespread belief in superstitions, spirits, sources of good fortune and the like serve practical ends, and although not all Thais will believe in them implicitly, there is a feeling that there is no harm in hedging one's bets. Much of it has nothing to do with Buddhism, but this does not detract from genuine religious faith. Buddhism tends to place emphasis on the ultimate transcendence of earthly cares, and thus there is room on the popular level for a multitude of beliefs and folk customs that can be relied upon to address more mundane matters — the Thais have a strong pragmatic streak.

Buddhism

The two most vital cohesive forces of Thai society are Buddhism and the monarchy.

More than 95 percent of Thais are Theravada Buddhists who not only profess but also practise the religion. The visitor need only go out into the street early in the morning to see saffron-robed monks receiving food alms from the people just as they have for hundreds of years. It is not a form of begging on the part of the monks; rather it is an opportunity for the giver to 'make merit' which is part and parcel of religious practice.

The Theravada faith, to give a simplified history, is the southern school of Buddhism as first preserved in Sri Lanka after the religion disappeared from India. It is contrasted with Mahayana Buddhism, or the northern school — so-called because it spread out from India via Nepal, Tibet and China and on to Korea, Vietnam and Japan.

The essence of all Buddhist teaching lies in the Four Noble Truths: *dukkha* (suffering and its inevitability), *samudaya* (the cause of suffering which is desire), *nirodha* (the cessation of suffering through the extinction of desire) and *magga* (the way to the cessation of suffering, i.e., the Noble Eightfold Path, namely, right understanding, right intention, right speech, right action, right livelihood, right effort, right mindfulness and right concentration).

The ultimate goal of the religion is *nirvana*, the extinction of suffering, which is reached through gaining merit in a long cycle of death and rebirth, the nature of the latter being dictated by *karma* or action. In practice most people aim simply for rebirth into a better existence, the state of *nirvana* being literally incomprehensible. Acts of gaining merit operate on the social as well as personal levels, and Thai society at its best exemplifies the Golden Rule 'doing unto others as you would have them do unto you'.

The focal point of worship in Theravada Buddhism is the Triratana, the Triple Gem comprising the Buddha, the Dhamma (the universal truth which he proclaimed) and the Sangha (the religious community and more particularly, the monkhood). The Triratana is ever present in Thai life; Buddha images abound in temples and homes, the universal truth (Dhamma) is preached in sermons and taught at schools, and monks are seen everywhere. Regarding the last, it is still common for most young Thai men to enter the monkhood at least once for a short period, generally the three months of Buddhist Lent.

The role of Buddhism in Thai life is also witnessed in the institution of the temple which historically, besides sustaining a monastic community, has served as village hostelry, village news, employment and information agency, school, hospital, dispensary and community centre.

While the tenets of Theravada Buddhism are faithfully adhered to, the religion is a tolerant one and in its practice in Thailand are incorporated certain elements of animism and Brahmanism. The inclusion of Brahmanic elements stems from the time when the Thais became heirs to the heritage of Angkor, and absorbed the practice of maintaining several Brahman priests at Court. The custom persists and today it is still priests of the tiny Brahman community who conduct the major royal rites and ceremonies.

Brahmanism in Thailand has made certain adaptations to become fully compatible with Buddhism, but the national faith is also tolerant of other religions which exist completely separately. There are sizeable communities of Christians, Muslims and Hindus, and Chinese temples, shrines and ancestral altars can be seen in nearly every city and town throughout the country.

The Monarchy

Since the founding of Sukhothai, Thai monarchs have directed the development of Thailand with a firm yet benign hand. Once known as 'Lords of Life', they formerly held absolute power and during the Ayutthaya period, influenced by the Khmer concept of a god-king, they assumed a semi-divine aura, becoming in effect both the symbol and embodiment of the nation.

The revolution of 1932 ended absolute monarchy and curtailed the political powers of the kings, but it in no way reduced the people's respect for them nor was their role downgraded to that of a mere figurehead. The monarchy is now as much a cohesive force as it ever was.

It is not easy for the visitor to understand the full extent of the people's respect for the royal family since there is no real parallel elsewhere in the world. There are, of course, other constitutional monarchies, but none function in quite the same way as in Thailand where the king is still a shaper of national welfare and continues to exercise a strong guiding influence in real and positive terms.

The present monarch, His Majesty King Bhumibol Adulyadej, Rama IX, ascended the throne in 1946 and, in what has become the dynasty's longest reign, the monarchy now enjoys the highest esteem of any time since King Chulalongkorn, Rama V (reigned 1868–1910).

The Thai Royal Family of the Chakri Dynasty

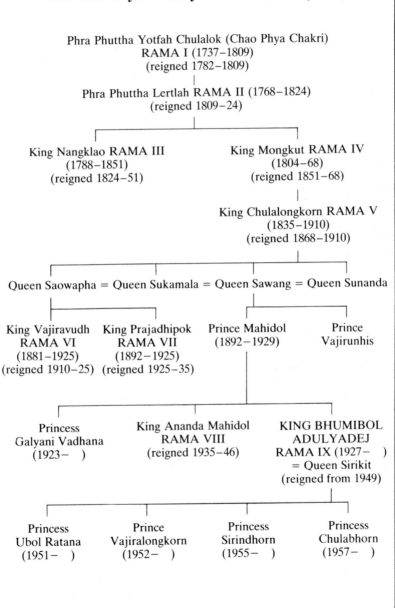

Phra Phuttha Yotfah Chulalok (Chao Phya Chakri)
RAMA I (1737–1809)
(reigned 1782–1809)

Phra Phuttha Lertlah RAMA II (1768–1824)
(reigned 1809–24)

King Nangklao RAMA III
(1788–1851)
(reigned 1824–51)

King Mongkut RAMA IV
(1804–68)
(reigned 1851–68)

King Chulalongkorn RAMA V
(1835–1910)
(reigned 1868–1910)

Queen Saowapha = Queen Sukamala = Queen Sawang = Queen Sunanda

King Vajiravudh
RAMA VI
(1881–1925)
(reigned 1910–25)

King Prajadhipok
RAMA VII
(1892–1925)
(reigned 1925–35)

Prince Mahidol
(1892–1929)

Prince
Vajirunhis

Princess
Galyani Vadhana
(1923–)

King Ananda Mahidol
RAMA VIII
(reigned 1935–46)

KING BHUMIBOL
ADULYADEJ
RAMA IX (1927–)
= Queen Sirikit
(reigned from 1949)

Princess
Ubol Ratana
(1951–)

Prince
Vajiralongkorn
(1952–)

Princess
Sirindhorn
(1955–)

Princess
Chulabhorn
(1957–)

Monsieur Du Chener Beltur, the French Ambassador, was granted an audience with His Majesty King Mongkut (King Rama IV) at Anantasamakom Hall in the Grand Palace on 25 November 1867. The painting is now at Chakri-Mahaprasad Hall in the Grand Palace.

A man of considerable personal accomplishment — yachtsman, artist, musician, photographer and poet — King Bhumibol works tirelessly for the prosperity of his people. In the onerous duties of the monarchy, he is supported by the immediate members of the royal family — Her Majesty Queen Sirikit, His Royal Highness Crown Prince Vajiralongkorn and his two younger sisters, Their Royal Highnesses Princess Maha Chakri Sirindhorn and Princess Chulabhorn.

While the king sets the example of an enlightened constitutional monarchy, he also reigns as Head of State, Upholder of Religions and Head of the Armed Forces. In consequence, a certain amount of the old royal ceremonial persists, along with a remarkable degree of the same public prestige as enjoyed under the rule of absolute royal power. His Majesty is popularly held to be sacred and inviolable. His portrait is seen everywhere and royal state occasions draw enormous public interest. This, along with frequent tours around the country, makes King Bhumibol one of the most highly visible personages in the country. The symbol and the man are uniquely combined in the role of monarch.

Government and Administration

The king and the capital are at the top of a pyramidal power structure, but since the Constitution of 1932 and its various successors it is recognized that sovereign power springs from three institutions: legislative power through the National Assembly, executive power through the Cabinet headed by a Prime Minister, and judicial power through the law courts which incorporate three levels of appeal.

The military remains a powerful influence and coups, successful and attempted, have been comparatively common. Increasingly in recent years, however, Thai-style democracy has become more secure and the flexing of military muscle is mostly unsuccessful without the people's support.

Centralized policy-shaping and administration is conducted through a system of ministries first organized along Western lines by King Chulalongkorn. Moving down the pyramid of government, Thailand is divided into 73 provinces, each with a governor and provincial capital. Administration is then further subdivided through district officers (*nai amphoe*) on down to the backbone of the nation, the rural village, where local affairs are presided over by a village headman (*pu yai ban*).

Art and Culture

As with other matters of national development, it has been Buddhism and the monarchy (through royal patronage) which have had the greatest influence on the major forms of classical Thai art, in particular sculpture, architecture and, in later periods, painting.

Sculpture has concentrated almost exclusively on images of the Buddha, created primarily not as art objects but as reminders of the faith. Besides Buddha images, sculpture has produced other religious statuary in the form of demonic and mythological creatures, some human, some animals and some fantastic hybrids, all of which adorn temples.

Architecture has achieved its greatest heights in temple buildings and *chedis* or pagodas. Common characteristics of temples are their multi-tiered roofs with sweeping eaves and carved pediments, and rich decorative detail inside and out. Pagodas are most common in the form of *chedis*, bell-shaped with graceful tapering spires, or as Khmer *prangs*, finger-like spires.

In addition to religious architecture, traditional Thai houses are distinctive. Made of teakwood panels enabling easy dismantling and reassembly at a new site, they rank among the world's earliest prefabricated buildings. They are distinguished by steep gabled roofs, elevation on stilts and, in the case of the finest houses, ornate woodcarving.

In painting, little survives prior to the late Ayutthaya period and what has survived mostly takes the form of temple murals or manuscript illustration, religious in nature and didactic in purpose. Common themes are episodes from lives of the Buddha and from the *Ramakien*, the Thai version of the ancient Indian epic, the *Ramayana* which, through the story of Prince Rama, recounts the struggle of good over evil. However, in between principal subjects and registers of worshipping divinities, artists managed to introduce cameo genre scenes showing aspects of ordinary Thai life, frequently with a well-developed sense of humour.

The *khon* masked dance drama, highly stylized and taking its plot exclusively from the *Ramakien*, was the classic form among the performing arts. *Lakhon* was a somewhat less formal dance drama, while *likay* was, and still is in some upcountry districts, a popular form of dramatic entertainment.

Khon performances continue to be staged at the National Theatre in Bangkok, though other once popular entertainments — shadow theatre and marionette shows — are now rarely seen.

Classical literature has been dominated by the *Ramakien* and a few other verse tales, along with popular folk stories designed for moral

Theatrical Extravaganza

*I*n Siam, all the important people have their own theatre and troupe of actors. His Majesty naturally has his own, which I can report on, having had the honour of an invitation to a show at the court. The theatre was in a yard adjacent to the throne room. Curtains of red and white silk, sculpted wainscotting and an infinite number of the immense cardboard cutouts at which the Siamese excel, made up the decor. To the right of the stage, decorated with rich tapestries, was his Majesty's box. The mandarins were bowing as low as they possibly could. In front of the stage, on the same level, was a huge dais furnished with European armchairs. The King had preceded us by a few minutes, and we had to bow to him and offer our humble respects before the pompous affair could begin.

The overture began with a shrill blast. The orchestra proceded to distinguish itself more by its earthshattering noise and the complete absence of harmony than by the variety of its repertoire. The same tune was played over and over for five hours, to the great delight of the king and his courtesans. I decided that all Siamese musical theory must revere this terrible noise; other concerts I have been forced to attend elsewhere consisted of the same unique and discordant notes. Finally the play began; a mob of actors hurled themselves on stage dressed in the most bizarre costumes imaginable. They were draped in gold brocade silk and proudly wore cone-shaped hats decorated with fake gems and glass beads on their heads. They threw coy and knowing glances our way. As for the play, I have never seen anything so simple. It was done almost completely in pantomime—original no doubt, but quite awkward, and all accompanied by a squalling choir placed close to the actors. I have no idea what the play was about; all I understood was a childish deer hunt. One actor, wearing a mask shaped like a deer's head, was caught, killed, taken away, cooked and eaten on stage, all this in less time than it takes to tell. However, the misfortune of this Siamese Actéon was not the last catastrophe of the drama. It continued for six hours until we took advantage of His Majesty's departure (we had been his guests, although we never exchanged a word).

Henri Mouhot, Voyages dans les Royaumes de Siam *(1868)*
translated by Sarah Jessup

guidance as well as entertainment. There was scarcely any prose writing until the 20th century and the novel is decidedly a latter-day form.

Influenced by Indian, Javanese, Chinese, Burmese, Malay and Khmer musical traditions, Thai classical music has a five-tone scale and is commonly played on a selection of wind and percussion instruments.

In the minor arts, decorative work is highly accomplished. Mother-of-pearl inlay and gold on black lacquer can be seen to excellent effect on doors and manuscript cabinets.

There is also a long tradition of handicrafts, with Chiang Mai being today the best-known centre for cottage industries. Products include cotton and silk weaving, woodcarving, silverware, bronzeware, basketry, jewellery and ceramics.

Thai Food

The Thais relish their food. That essential trait *sanuk*, taking pleasure in life, finds full expression in dining, and Thais have a rare fondness for their national cuisine.

Most visitors share this delight in Thai food and find it one of the world's truly great culinary treats, full of richness and variety. Yet pleasure in eating only partially accounts for the Thais' creativity in cooking. There is also the matter of ingredients and in this respect Thailand is most fortunate, with both the land and the surrounding sea yielding rich harvests. The staple, rice, grows in abundance as do the numerous varieties of vegetables, fruit, herbs and spices so beloved to the Thai palate. Pork and poultry are favoured meats, while many species of fish and crustaceans, both freshwater and from the sea, are popular and plentiful.

The basis of a Thai meal is, of course, rice. This is commonly steamed although it can be made into noodles, while glutinous or sticky rice is preferred with some specialities. Accompanying are four or five main dishes featuring vegetables, meat, seafood, egg, fish and soup according to choice. Utensils are a fork and spoon and after helping yourself to a scoop of rice, you take small amounts from the other dishes as taste and appetite dictate. Like Chinese dining, it is something of a communal affair.

Besides the rice and other dishes, absolutely essential to any Thai meal are the sauces taken to give additional spice. For the novice there can be a bewildering number of these, but the most common are *nam pla*, a liquid fish sauce which is extremely salty, and *nam prik*, also a liquid but with pieces of chillies, garlic, shrimp curd, sugar and lime. Care should be taken with the latter as the chillies can be very hot.

Although Thais generally prefer hot, spicy food, not all dishes are

Mudras of Buddha

Statues of the Buddha show him in one of the four basic postures: walking, standing, sitting and reclining (the last being the Buddha on his deathbed at the moment of attaining nirvana). In addition, individual images depict *mudras* or hand gestures, each of which has a special meaning. Among the most common are:

Bhumisparsa Mudra (Calling the Earth to Witness) — Also known as Subduing Mara (*Maravijaya*). Seated as for meditation but the *vajrasana* or 'adamantine posture' has the legs crossed so that each foot rests on the opposite thigh, soles upward. The left hand lies in the lap, palm upward, while the right hand lies over the right knee, fingers pointing to the ground. In this fashion the Buddha called the earth as witness to his goodness when challenged by Mara.

Samadhi (Meditation) — The Buddha is seated in the *virasana* or 'hero posture' in which legs are crossed, folded one on top of the other. The hands lie in the lap, palms upward.

Vitarka Mudra (Teaching) — One or both hands held parallel to the body at chest height with the thumb and forefinger joined. Shown in the standing figure.

Abhaya Mudra (Dispelling Fear) — The gesture of giving protection or calming, shown in the standing or walking Buddha and made with the right hand, or occasionally with both hands. The upper arm is held close to the body, the forearm is outstretched at almost a right angle and the hand is held palm forward with the fingers pointing upward.

Varada Mudra (Charity) — In this gesture the arms of the standing Buddha are held straight down by the sides of the body with the palms of the hands facing outward.

Buddha Images

In theory all Buddha images should be the same, for they all represent Siddhartha Gautama. However, no likeness of the Enlightened One was made during his lifetime. As a result, while all statues have common elements, features have been interpreted differently. The following is a rough guide to the identification of sculpted Buddha heads from the major Thai schools of sculpture:

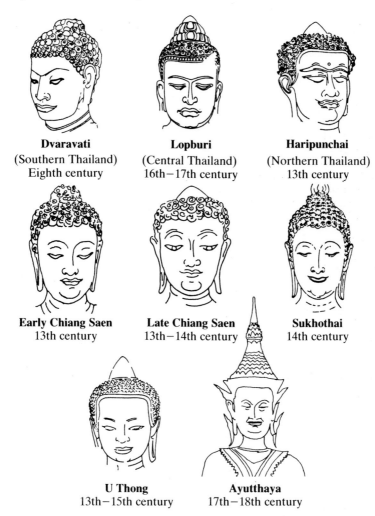

Dvaravati
(Southern Thailand)
Eighth century

Lopburi
(Central Thailand)
16th–17th century

Haripunchai
(Northern Thailand)
13th century

Early Chiang Saen
13th century

Late Chiang Saen
13th–14th century

Sukhothai
14th century

U Thong
13th–15th century

Ayutthaya
17th–18th century

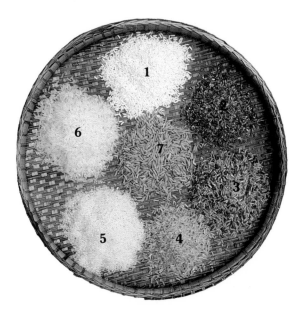

Thai rices:
1. *'Kao-neo', sticky rice*
2. *'Kao daeng', red rice*
3. *Mixed grains unpolished rice*
4. *Unpolished rice*
5. *Lower grade broken rice*
6. *'Kao hom-male', high-grade fragrant rice*
7. *Unhusked rice*

Thai peppers:
1. *Plik Chi Fa Haeng*
2. *Plik Leung (sweetest)*
3. *Plik Kii Nu Haeng*
4. *Plik Chi Fa Daeng*
5. *Plik Thai Sot*
6. *Plik Thai Haeng (black pepper)*
7. *Plik Noom*
8. *Plik Kii Nu (hottest)*

equally fiery. There are grades of hotness, hence the sauces to add extra fire if desired. Thai food, while never bland, can be modulated to suit most palates. (A word of warning, however; watch out for *prik- ·kee-noo*, tiny little green or red chillies which are hotter than hot.)

In the soup department, Thailand's great contribution to the culinary arts is *tom yam*. This is a sour soup which can be made with various kinds of meat or fish but its most famous version is made with prawns, *tom yam goong*. The basic broth is flavoured with lemon grass, citrus leaves, lime juice, fish sauce and hot chillies.

Other common methods of Thai food preparation include curries, and the stir-fried dishes which are cooked in a *wok* with pork fat oil, pepper and plenty of garlic. Then there is a wide choice of salad preparations (*yam*) made with just vegetables or with different kinds of meat or fish and mixed with distinctive flavourings such as lemon grass, fish sauce and such like, plus lime juice to give a characteristic sourness.

For dessert there are many sorts of local sweet goodies — *kanoms* — often of a coconut flavour, and a vast array of tropical fruits, a minor gourmet discovery in themselves (see page 126).

Below is a small sampling of dishes which should provide a tasty introduction to some of the more common Thai specialities.

Soup Apart from *tom yam goong* mentioned above, try *gaeng liang fak thong* (pumpkin and coconut); *gaeng chud* (consomme with stuffed mushrooms — very easy on the palate); or *gai tom kah* (chicken cooked in coconut milk).

Seafood *Gaeng kalee goong* (lobster and prawn curry); *goong pad phed* (fried prawns with chilli paste); *pad preo wan goong* (sweet and sour shrimps); *poo cha* (stuffed crab shells); *hoh mok hoy* (steamed mussels); *pla mueg pad prik* (fried squid with hot sauce); *pla khao lard prik* (fried garoupa with chilli sauce); *gaeng kua nuer* (fish and vegetable curry); *pla pad king* (seabass with fresh ginger).

Poultry *Gai obb bai toey* (fried chicken in pandan leaves); *gaeng phed* (duck and vegetables); *gaeng phed gai* (curried chicken); *tom kem gai* (chicken casserole).

Rice and Noodles *Khao obb sapparod* (fried rice in pineapple); *khao pad prik* (fried curried rice); *khao soi* (curried noodles).

Meat *Kaeb moo* (crispy fried pork); *gaeng kiew wan* (green beef curry); *yam neau* (Thai beef salad); *pad luke chin* (steamed pork balls with vegetables).

Vegetables *Pad kow-port onn gab gai* (baby corn with chicken); *pak tom ka-ti* (vegetables boiled in coconut milk); *pak dong* (pickled vegetables).

Desserts *Sang-kaya gab kanoon* (coconut custard with jack fruit); *khao neo mamuang* (sticky rice and mango).

When it comes to places to eat, Bangkok has a wealth of restaurants in all categories and price ranges from the corner noodle stall (safe and good simple food) right up to the plush deluxe hotel establishments. For an authentic Thai meal the visitor is best advised to avoid the large restaurants also offering Thai dancing and cultural shows, as these places generally present menus tempered to what is believed to be *farang* (foreign) tastes. Head instead for the unpretentious spots where the locals go.

In upcountry areas restaurants may look pretty basic, but generally the food is far better than the surroundings suggest. Again, the best guide is to go to places the Thais favour.

Conduct

While the Thais are in general a tolerant and easy-going people, full of hospitality towards the stranger, they do, like other nationalities, place stress on certain social customs. These the visitor will do well to follow so as to avoid embarrassment and to show respect.

Thais regard the head as the highest part of the body, figuratively as well as literally. It is, therefore, considered an insult to touch or pat anyone other than intimates and small children on the head. In like manner the feet are the lowest part of the body and it is extremely rude to point with one's feet, step over a reclining body or kick anyone.

As mentioned, both Buddhism and the monarchy are highly regarded, and proper respect should be shown to all Buddha images (old or new, ruined or complete) and to anything (money, documents, etc.) that bears a likeness of the king.

Buddhist monks are also deeply revered and should be accorded extreme politeness. Moreover, because of vows of celibacy, a monk must not be touched nor even brushed against by a woman.

When visiting temples one should dress in a way that will not cause offence — bare shoulders, short shorts and other provocative forms of attire should be avoided. Shoes may be worn when walking in a temple compound but must be removed when entering a chapel containing Buddha images. (Shoes are also removed when you visit a private house.)

To lose one's temper is considered by Thais to be the height of bad manners and achieves absolutely nothing. If one is involved in a dispute, one should remain calm and never shout no matter how much provocation there might be. It is worth remembering at all times that fundamental Thai attitude summed up in the phrase *mai pen rai*, which means 'never mind' or 'it doesn't matter'.

Although not actually involving possible social blunders, two other points are worthy of note. The correct form of greeting is the *wai*, which is performed by placing the palms of the hands together, raising them to the face with the finger tips at eye level and inclining the head slightly forward. Thais do not expect foreigners to *wai* but are pleased when such courtesy is shown. Finally, it is the usual practice to address people by their first, given name (or nickname) and not their surname. This holds true with friends or someone met for the first time. The custom is especially convenient for the foreigner since most Thai surnames are polysyllabic tongue-twisters.

General Information for Travellers

Getting There

By Air There are over 40 international airlines serving Bangkok's Don Muang International Airport. Thai International, the national flag carrier, flies to Bangkok from the United States, Australia (Sydney, Melbourne, Brisbane and Perth), London, as well as a number of other major European, Middle Eastern and Asian cities.

Regionally, Bangkok is easily reached from Hong Kong (nearly 12 daily flights, various airlines), Beijing, Taipei, Manila, Singapore, Jakarta, Kuala Lumpur, Penang, Rangoon, Dhaka, Calcutta and Kathmandu.

Among the more exotic embarkation points are Kunming, in southwestern China, Hanoi and Vientiane, although at present the latter two are rarely accessible to Westerners.

By Rail Comfortable and inexpensive express trains connect Bangkok with Penang, Malaysia (overnight) and Singapore (three days and three nights, including an overnight stop in Penang).

By Road At present, the only overland entry, aside from the Penang–Bangkok express train, is by two roads that cross the Malaysian border in southernmost Thailand. Most tourists traverse the border by taxi, as few private or hired cars are permitted to cross due to insurance technicalities.

Visas

Visitors from most Western nations can obtain a 15-day, non-extendable transit visa upon arrival in Thailand. For travellers anticipating a longer stay, tourist visas, valid for 60 days, should be obtained prior to departure. Application for a 30-day extension costs ฿500 (about US$18). Those planning to study or do business in Thailand must obtain a non-immigrant visa, valid for 90 days but generally not extendable. There is a ฿100/day fine levied at the airport on those who overstay the term of their visa. All persons who stay in Thailand for a total of 90 days or longer in one calendar year must obtain a tax clearance certificate before leaving the country, whether or not they have earnings or income to declare.

Customs

Customs formalities tend to be rather cursory for Western tourists. Do not be daunted by the entry forms handed out upon arrival asking for the declaration of all watches, radios, etc. Personal effects in

reasonable quantity need not be meticulously declared. Cash,
travellers' cheques and other monetary instruments with a cumulative
value of more than US$10,000 must be declared, however.

No Thai cultural relics classified as antiques may be taken out of
the country without a certificate from the Fine Arts Department. (This
restriction does not apply to antiques originating elsewhere, such as
Burma or China, but purchased in Thailand.) In addition, *no* Buddha
image, whether ancient or modern, may be exported. Travellers
should also be warned that there are harsh penalties awaiting anyone
caught smuggling illegal drugs and other contraband into or out of
Thailand.

Health

There are no particular vaccination requirements, but innoculation
against typhoid and tetanus is recommended, as is gamma globulin,
helpful in alleviating the symptoms of hepatitis A (avoid eating raw
freshwater shellfish).

Parts of Thailand, particularly the mountainous areas in the north
and the Laotian and Kampuchean border areas (including the Mekong
River), are host to chloroquine-resistant strains of malaria. Fansidar,
once widely prescribed as a preventive, has been found to cause severe
allergic reactions in some people; consult your doctor.

Do not drink water from the tap anywhere in Thailand — bottled
water and soft drinks are readily available throughout the country. Ice
at roadside stands should be eschewed, and care taken when eating
seafood and raw vegetables outside of Bangkok. Most restaurants,
however, both in Bangkok and upcountry, maintain reasonably high
standards of hygiene, and undue caution need not inhibit one's
enjoyment of Thailand's culinary offerings.

Visitors from the temperate zones should be particularly alert to
the dangers of heat exhaustion and sunburn.

Health care in the major urban areas is excellent, and private
hospitals in Bangkok are staffed mostly by Western-educated, English-
speaking doctors.

Money

Currency The standard unit of currency is the *baht* (฿), which is
divided into 100 *satang*. Coins include 25- and 50-*satang*, and the much
more common 1-, 5- and 10-*baht* pieces. Bills come in 10, 20, 50, 100
and 500 *baht* denominations.

Exchange Currencies and travellers' cheques can be exchanged at
most (but not all) banks and hotels. Many banks have special foreign

exchange windows which stay open evenings and weekends.

Credit cards Internationally recognized credit cards, such as Visa, MasterCard and American Express, are accepted at many of the more expensive hotels, restaurants and shops in Bangkok and at most first-class hotels in the smaller cities. Otherwise, cash is the primary means of exchange.

Tipping Outside of the major hotels and restaurants, tipping is not a common practice in Thailand. It is customary at restaurants, however, to leave the small change, generally ฿5–20, for the waiters.

Transportation

Air Travel Two local carriers, Thai Airways and Bangkok Air, operate a fleet of B-737, Airbus, Avro and Shorts jet and turboprop aircraft to a wide array of domestic and regional destinations. Comparatively low fares make air transport a viable option for travel within Thailand, though you miss much of the scenery along the way. Note that at Don Muang the domestic terminal is about two kilometres (1.5 miles) from the international departures building; be sure to specify which terminal you want to your taxi driver in Bangkok.

Trains Bangkok is the hub of Thailand's excellent rail system, which radiates out in six major trunk and branch lines to serve nearly every major population centre in the country. The trains are comfortable and clean, fares are inexpensive and even the food served is good; there is no more pleasant or leisurely way to see the countryside.

There are three classes. Passengers in air-conditioned first-class coaches sleep two to a compartment; bring along a light sweater, as the air-conditioning can make things uncomfortably chilly. Second class offers air-conditioned and fan-cooled sleepers (reclining seats in the air-conditioned coaches, convertible couchettes otherwise); lower berths are preferred as they are more spacious and the window can be opened — very romantic on moonlit, tropical nights. Third-class seats are quite cheap, but recommended only for short hauls.

Tickets should be booked in advance (at least a week for the more popular routes such as Bangkok–Chiang Mai, especially when travelling on weekends and holidays). Bookings can be made through most Bangkok tour agencies, or at the Advance Booking office at Hualampong Station (see page 213 for details).

Buses Serving nearly every settlement from big cities to backwoods hamlets, Thailand's ubiquitous buses are a vital link in the nation's transportation network. Luxury air-conditioned coaches, some equipped with TV and video-cassette players, ply the routes between major cities, while a fascinating array of vehicles, large and small, new and antique, in various states of disrepair, serve destinations of lesser importance. In many cases, unless you have hired a car and driver, buses are the only way to reach a given locale. But while Thailand's roads are generally very good, her drivers do not enjoy as favourable a reputation. Accidents are altogether too frequent, and many involve drivers working for private bus companies. Theft can also be a problem — keep your valuables on your person, especially on overnight trips. Armed highway robbery is another occasional night-time hazard along some of the less-travelled mountain roads in the north and southwest; incidents of banditry are becoming increasingly rare, however.

Ordinary local and regional buses seem to be less prone to misfortune and are often the only way to get where you are going, precluding other means of transport. For day excursions from Bangkok and Chiang Mai in particular, buses will be your primary option, and for such purposes are generally safe and reliable.

Communications

Thailand's postal system is quite reliable for outgoing mail. Both local and long-distance telephone systems are quite efficient; there is international direct dialling in some areas.

Telex and facsimile services are widely available — many hotels maintain business centres where these and other services, such as copying, are available.

The most convenient way to send purchases home is to arrange for the shop to handle wrapping and mailing for you. If you choose to mail your own parcels, it is best to go to Bangkok's main post office on New Road, which offers a packing service. Note that there is a 10-kilogram (22-pound) limit on the weight of any one item sent through the mail.

Language

In Bangkok, most hotel service staff, many shopkeepers, some waiters and waitresses and a few taxi drivers speak or understand some English. Upcountry, English speakers are harder to come by, although in such popular tourist destinations as Chiang Mai language is less of a problem.

The most widely-used language in Thailand is, of course, Thai. Most Westerners find it very difficult to master, but learning a few useful phrases (Thai Vocabulary, page 186) will come in handy and endear you greatly to your hosts.

Besides the numerous hilltribe dialects, the non-Thai languages most often encountered are Lao (actually a dialect of Thai) and Khmer in the northeast, and Chinese (Teochew and Mandarin dialects).

What to Pack

Clothing Light cotton and linen clothing are best suited to Thailand's tropical climate. Thais dress informally but neatly — the same will be expected of the visitor. Shorts, short skirts and other revealing outfits are suitable as beachwear only. Flip-flops should be likewise eschewed. Since shoes are always removed before entering private homes and temple sanctuaries, a comfortable pair of slip-on loafers is recommended. For jungle treks, bring along a pair of broken-in walking shoes or sneakers.

Evening wear need not be too formal; more elaborate attire, such as tie and jacket, is rarely necessary except at Bangkok's poshest hotel restaurants or at formal receptions.

Medicine and Toiletries Both Western and high-quality domestic brands of toothpaste, deodorant, shaving supplies, shampoo, tampons, sanitary napkins, cosmetics and other toiletries are widely available.

For the sake of convenience, bring prescription medicines, vitamins, sunscreen oil, mosquito repellent, cold and digestive medicines and other regularly used first-aid remedies. However, a wide array of prescription and non-prescription medicines and medical supplies are readily available.

Liquor and Tobacco Western, Chinese and local wines and spirits are widely available, but heavily taxed. Nevertheless, the most popular domestic whiskey, Mekhong, is still comparatively inexpensive by Western standards. Two local brands of beer, Kloster and Singha, are sold throughout the country and are comparable to good German brew.

The Government has a monopoly on tobacco, and both domestically produced as well as foreign cigarettes are (legally) available.

Film Most major American and Japanese brands of film are on sale throughout Thailand, but some types and sizes are hard to find, so it is wise to bring along an ample supply. Same-day (and even one-hour) developing is available for most film types, with the notable exception of Kodachrome, which must be sent to Australia for processing.

Electrical Appliances Electric current is 220v ac, 50 cycles. Both round and square plugs are used, so it is advisable to pack an adapter. Local AM and FM radio stations operate in the same frequency ranges as in the United States and Europe.

Reading Material Bangkok boasts three English-language dailies, the *Bangkok Post*, *The Nation* and *The World*. The *International Herald Tribune* can be found in most hotel lobby bookstores and newstands along with a wide selection Western magazines and periodicals. There are a number of excellent English and other foreign-language bookstores in Bangkok, notably Asia Books on Sukhumvit Road between Sois 15 and 17.

Climate

Thailand's climate can be roughly divided into three seasons. The warm and dry season, from mid-October to early March, is the best time for travel. December and January are the coolest months, although temperatures in Bangkok, which has been rated as the world's hottest metropolis, reach 32°C (90°F) nearly every day of the year. Visitors to Chiang Mai or the Northeast during the cooler months would be well-advised to pack a sweater or light jacket.

Flooding can be a problem in Bangkok during September, the wettest month, but the rainy season (from mid-May through mid-October) is actually not a bad time to visit Thailand; heavy, prolonged rainfalls are rare, and temperatures are generally moderate throughout this period. On the other hand, while sunshine abounds during the hot and dry season (March to mid-May), the heat can become oppressive as temperatures climb to over 39°C (100°F) and the usually lush, green countryside is reduced to an arid, brown brushland.

Peninsular southern Thailand has a climate with little seasonal variation. Daytime temperatures hover around 32°C (90°F) and dip to 24°C (75°F) at night. Evening rainshowers occur throughout the year.

A one-kilogram Burmese ruby rough is inspected by a gem merchant.

Bangkok
7 ft (2 m)13°45′ N 100°28′ E 37 years

	Temperature °F				Temperature °C			Precipitation	
	Highest recorded	Average daily		Lowest recorded	Highest recorded	Average daily		Lowest recorded	Average monthly	
		max.	min.			max.	min.		in	mm
J	100	89	68	55	38	32	20	13	0.3	8
F	106	91	72	56	41	33	22	13	0.8	20
M	104	93	75	57	40	34	24	14	1.4	36
A	106	95	77	67	41	35	25	19	2.3	58
M	106	93	77	71	41	34	25	22	7.8	198
J	100	91	76	70	38	33	24	21	6.3	160
J	101	90	76	71	38	32	24	22	6.3	160
A	99	90	76	72	37	32	24	22	6.9	175
S	98	89	76	69	37	32	24	21	12.0	305
O	100	88	75	64	38	31	24	18	8.1	206
N	99	87	72	56	37	31	22	13	2.6	66
D	100	87	68	52	38	31	20	.11	0.2	5

Chiang Mai
1030 ft (314 m) 18°47′ N 98°59′ E 13 years

	Temperature °F				Temperature °C			Precipitation	
	Highest recorded	Average daily		Lowest recorded	Highest recorded	Average daily		Lowest recorded	Average monthly	
		max.	min.			max.	min.		in	mm
J	97	84	56	43	36	29	13	6	0	0
F	97	89	58	49	36	32	14	9	0.4	10
M	102	94	63	55	39	34	17	13	0.3	8
A	108	97	71	59	43	36	22	15	1.4	36
M	106	94	73	67	41	34	23	19	4.8	122
J	100	90	74	69	38	32	23	21	4.4	112
J	99	88	74	66	37	31	23	19	8.4	213
A	99	88	74	70	37	31	23	21	7.6	193
S	96	88	73	65	36	31	23	18	9.8	249
O	96	87	70	60	36	31	21	16	3.7	94
N	99	86	66	54	37	30	19	12	1.2	31
D	97	83	59	43	36	28	15	6	0.5	13

Shopping

Thailand's department stores, shops and market stalls offer a wide array of interesting and beautiful items, with quite a few bargains to boot. Bangkok is, naturally, the focus of most shoppers' attentions, but the best bargains in silver, hilltribe jewellery and handicrafts, embroidery, woodcarving, lacquer and even Burmese antiques are found upcountry, notably in Chiang Mai.

With the exception of department stores and the largest shops, bargaining is not only practised but usually expected. With patience, a friendly smile and courteous determination you can expect discounts of 20−30 percent. Below are listed some general rules to follow when shopping in Thailand's markets and shops:

Touts are to be avoided. Such people are paid commissions by certain shops for introducing customers.

Receipts should be obtained for all purchases and, in the case of gems or antiques, you should ask for a certificate of authentication.

As a simple safety precaution, it is advisable not to carry more cash than you expect to use that day. Make use of hotel safety deposit boxes.

Major credit cards are accepted in the bigger establishments and shops specializing in the tourist trade.

Many shops can package and ship purchases to your home address. If this is done, it is advisable to take out insurance coverage which the shop should be able to arrange.

Best buys for the intrepid shopper include:

Thai Silk Handwoven and available in a wide variety of weights, colours and patterns, silk may be purchased either by length or as ready-made items of clothing.

Thai Cotton Like silk, handwoven cotton is a traditional craft in rural areas. The cloth is ideal for both ladies' and men's clothing, and is especially suitable for Bangkok's hot, sticky climate.

Gems and Jewellery Bangkok is a major world centre for coloured gem stones which are both mined locally and imported for cutting. Best of the local stones are ruby and sapphire. Gems may be purchased either individually or as ready-made pieces of jewellery. Look for clear colour and good cutting as well as size. All good shops will give certificates of authentication.

Silverware Good price and high quality due to the skill of Thai silversmiths in both high and low relief work makes silver a good buy. Recommended items include bowls, cigarette boxes and the chunky silver jewellery produced by Thailand's northern hilltribes.

Nielloware Made of silver inlaid with black alloy, the craft dates back to the 17th century and the various products (from jewellery to cigarette boxes) are unusual and attractive.

Bronzeware The casting of Buddha images, gongs and bowls has been carried out for many centuries. Popular buys include bronze cutlery sets, generally with rosewood handles.

Woodcarving An enormous range of items are carved out of solid teak. Animal figures (notably elephants), salad bowls, trays and so on are popular portable buys, while teakwood furniture is good and comparatively inexpensive. Most shops can arrange for the packaging and shipping of large items.

Lacquerware Items made from covering a bamboo frame with many layers of resin which, when dry, are painted and polished to a high gloss include boxes, chests, trays, small tables, and decorative plates. Colour schemes are black and gold, or orange, green and yellow.

Celadon Pottery The art of ceramics flourished in Thailand during the Sukhothai period when King Ramkamhaeng settled Chinese potters in the country. The craft subsequently went into decline but has been revived in recent years. The distinctive high-fired green pottery is available in many forms: lamp bases, vases, etc.

Bangkok

Located on a flat alluvial plain traversed by the Chao Phraya River some 40 kilometres (25 miles) upstream from its outlet into the Gulf of Thailand, Bangkok is an unprepossessing city on first impression. It sprawls monstrously, its traffic congestion is notorious and its lack of a definable downtown area inhibits easy orientation and ready appreciation of attractions. Yet Bangkok is full of wondrous sights and behind the façade it remains first and foremost an oriental city; the city's Western looks and styles are mere borrowings and adaptations, disguising, not supplanting, the indigenous.

It requires a little effort to discover the charm of the place, but the task is well-rewarded. What can at first seem a monotonous urban pancake then reveals itself as a city diverse in moods and looks. The area around the Grand Palace stands, for example, in marked contrast to the new royal district in Dusit where Chitralada Palace, the present residence of the Royal Family, is located; and Chinatown, with its air of impending chaos and frenetic commercial activity, presents a very different picture from the modern business and shopping quarters centred on Silom and Sukhumvit roads.

Bangkok is a place to explore and enjoy the delight of discovery. Its many magnificent sights are not so much monumental as surprising. Incongruity often adds to the appeal. It soon becomes evident that the city has a remarkable wealth of historical and cultural attractions surviving in a sea of latter-day development.

Bangkok is a gourmet's (and gourmand's, for that matter) paradise and probably offers more restaurants to the square mile than anywhere else. And it is not simply the sheer number of establishments: there is also excellent quality (not necessarily expensive) and great variety, with styles of cuisine ranging from hot spicy Thai cooking to just about any national culinary offering you care to name.

Shopping opportunities are plenty and best buys include silk and cotton, custom tailoring, gems and jewellery, leathergoods, art objects and a host of handicrafts.

Finally, the nightlife is almost legendary and hardly needs any introduction. The choice of activities is wide open and ranges from go-go bars to sophisticated nightclubs, from Thai boxing matches to discos.

Getting around Bangkok

Bangkok's streets can be quite intimidating to the first-time visitor with their Los Angeles-style sprawl, New York-style gridlock and Romestyle drivers. To top it off, streets and lanes are arranged in haphazard fashion and some seem to change name at every major intersection. However, and with a little practice, the intrepid traveller will quickly master the art of getting around in Thailand's capital city.

Taxis For both the independent traveller and the tour-group member taking advantage of free time, taxis are the most oft-used means of conveyance in Bangkok. Taxi cabs are not equipped with meters. Instead, the fare is negotiated *prior* to getting in. (The exception to the bargaining rule is hotel taxis, whose fixed rates may be as much as two times the going 'street' rate.)

The fare depends on distance, your bargaining skills and time of day — rush hours add ฿10–20. The minimum is generally around ฿30 for very short distances; a ride from the Sukhumvit area to the Grand Palace will cost about ฿80-100. Expect to pay about ฿180 (฿300 for hotel taxi) to and from the airport. Once the fare is agreed upon, there should be no additions or surcharges; tipping is not customary.

Few taxi drivers speak English, so have your destination, as well as hotel name and address, written out in Thai.

Tuk-tuks A more direct encounter with Bangkok traffic can be had by flagging down one of the city's swarm of motorized trishaws, called *tuk-tuks* in Thai (presumably an onomatopoeic designation). Marginally cheaper than taxis, these vehicles are popular with the locals for short hops and with tourists for joy-rides. *Tuk-tuk* drivers have a penchant for wild bursts of speed on the straightaways, and seem to draw sustenance from the exhaust pipes of smoke-belching buses idling at red lights; but try it once, for the experience. Fares start at ฿20.

Pedicabs Now banned in Bangkok, human-powered pedicabs (*samlors*) still ply the streets of most upcountry towns and cities. Again, agree on the fare before setting off — ฿10-20 is the normal range. *Samlor* seats are quite narrow. For the sake of comfort, those of medium build or larger would be well-advised to hire one *samlor* per adult, except for very short distances.

Buses Bangkok has an excellent and relatively easy-to-use city bus system. The fare for ordinary buses is ฿2 (no distance limitation); fares for air-conditioned buses range from ฿5 to 20, depending on the distance. Many of the air-conditioned bus routes cover quite a bit of the city — a comfortable and inexpensive way to take in the town.

Background

Bangkok was founded as the Thai capital in 1782 by King Rama I. Prior to that it had been little more than a customs post and small

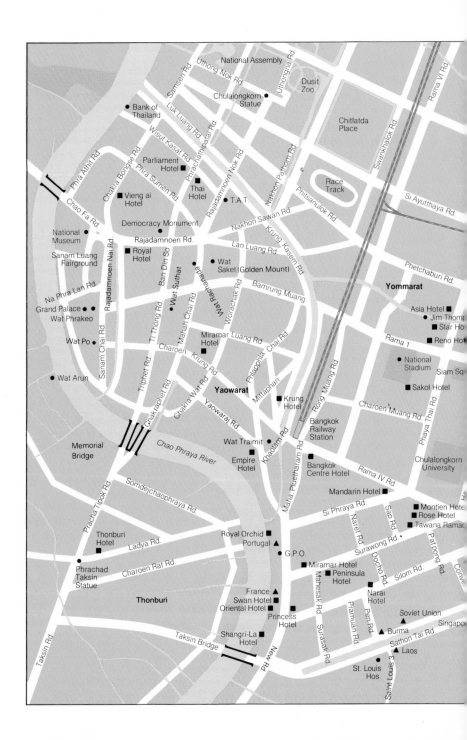

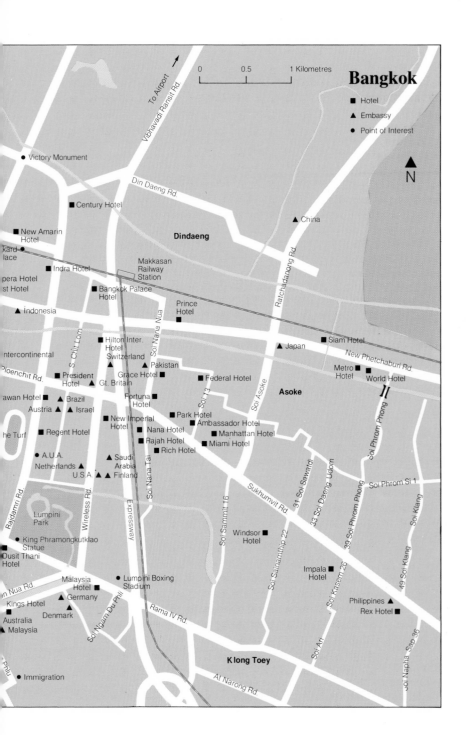

Bangkok

■ Hotel
▲ Embassy
● Point of Interest

N

0   0.5   1 Kilometres

To Airport
Vibhavadi Ransit Rd.

● Victory Monument

Din Daeng Rd.

■ Century Hotel

Dindaeng

■ New Amarin
Hotel

kard
lace

■ Indra Hotel

pera Hotel
st Hotel

■ Bangkok Palace
Hotel

Makkasan
Railway
Station

Prince
Hotel ■

▲ Indonesia

▲ China

Ratchadapong Rd.

■ Siam Hotel

New Phetchaburi Rd.

▲ Japan

ntercontinental

S. Chit Lom

■ Hilton Inter.
Hotel
Switzerland ▲

Soi Nana Nua

▲ Pakistan

Ploenchit Rd.

■ President
Hotel

Grace Hotel ■

▲ Gt. Britain

■ Federal Hotel

Asoke

Metro
Hotel ■

■ World Hotel

awan Hotel ■
Austria ▲

▲ Brazil
▲ Israel

Fortuna
Hotel ■

Soi 13

Soi Asoke

he Turf

■ Regent Hotel

■ New Imperial
Hotel

■ Park Hotel
■ Ambassador Hotel

■ Manhattan Hotel

■ Nana Hotel

■ Rajah Hotel

■ Miami Hotel

● A.U.A.
Netherlands ▲
U.S.A. ▲

▲ Saudi
Arabia
▲ Finland

■ Rich Hotel

Soi Phrom Phong

Soi Phrom Si 1

Soi Klang

Rajdamri Rd.

Lumpini
Park

Wireless Rd.

Soi Nana Tai

Expressway

Soi Sammit 16

Sukhumvit Rd.

31 Soi Sawardi

33 Soi Daeng-Udom

39 Soi Phrom Phong

49 Soi Klang

● King Phramongkutklao
Statue

Dusit Thani
Hotel

Malaysia
Hotel ■

● Lumpini Boxing
Stadium

Windsor ■
Hotel

Soi Sainamthip 22

Impala ■
Hotel

Soi Kasem 25

Philippines ▲
Rex Hotel ■

Soi Napha-Sap 36

n Nua Rd.

Kings Hotel
■

▲ Germany

Australia
▲ Malaysia

▲ Denmark

Soi Ngam Du Phli

Rama IV Rd.

Philu

● Immigration

Klong Toey

At Narong Rd.

Soi Ari

settlement of Chinese traders. When Rama I mapped out his plans for the new capital, it was his intention to build a city that would reflect the lost glory of Ayutthaya and restore national pride (see page 21). The former capital had been an island city and so Bangkok was to follow suit. As the site stands on a broad loop in the river, it required only the cutting of canals in concentric arcs on the east flank to bring the water all around.

The royal palace had traditionally been the physical and symbolic heart of the capital. Accordingly, the Chinese traders were moved away from prime real estate on the banks of the river and the Grand Palace.

Bangkok continued to look to the model of Ayutthaya throughout the first three reigns of the Chakri Dynasty, each monarch adding to and embellishing the city until it was one of the biggest and finest in the East. A radical shift in emphasis came in the mid-19th century, beginning with the reign of King Mongkut, Rama IV (see page 21). He ceased to look to the models of the past and instead sought to modernize the nation (and for all practical purposes that meant Bangkok) by opening up Thailand to the outside world. Perhaps the single most significant turning point for Bangkok came in 1857 when King Mongkut ordered the construction of the first roads capable of taking wheeled traffic. The first of these, New Road, was completed in 1862.

The expansion of Bangkok has continued apace ever since. Since 1900, the metropolitan area has expanded from 300 to more than 1,500 square kilometres (115 to 580 square miles) and the population has grown from an estimated 460,000 to over six million.

Inevitably, in meeting the demands of such phenomenal growth, the balance and symmetry of the city has been upset. Nearly all the canals have now been filled in to make way for motor vehicles and building development has been dictated more by pragmatic considerations than aesthetic concerns.

Prior to World War II new building in the capital mostly enhanced the cityscape, albeit following colonial rather than pure Thai design (for example, the headquarters of the East Asiatic Company next to the Oriental Hotel). But in the 1950s and '60s expansion was so rapid that practical demands outweighed all else. Hence the eminently functional and incredibly ugly shophouse, rows of three- to four-storey concrete retail outlets-cum-residences of unrelieved monotony.

It was not just the building which altered the appearance of Bangkok and disguised much of its original beauty. As the city expanded the focal point shifted and gradually, with little or inadequate planning, any kind of downtown centre was lost in the haphazard sprawl.

In light of Bangkok's rapid growth it is not so much the modern veneer that is surprising, but rather the number of monuments of the past that have survived. The historic sights may be partly veiled yet they manage to coexist with the latter-day manifestations of this vibrant and exuberant city.

Sights

The Old Royal City

The Grand Palace and Wat Phra Keo
(Open daily, admission to Wat Phra Keo ฿100, includes entry ticket to Vimanmek Throne Hall.) The main entrance to the massive white battlements enclosing Wat Phra Keo and the buildings of the Grand Palace is on Na Phralan Road. This complex indisputably tops any sightseeing list for Bangkok.

The Grand Palace
Here is the perfect introduction to the whole matter of Thailand: the Buddhist faith, regal grandeur and a deep respect for tradition. Though no longer the royal residence, and used only on special state occasions, the Grand Palace nevertheless remains the symbolic heart of the capital. Moreover, Wat Phra Keo, occupying one corner of the extensive compound, enshrines the nation's most revered Buddha image and is still the principal royal chapel.

The earliest palace buildings date from 1782, the year Bangkok became the capital, while succeeding monarchs added extensively to the work begun by Rama I. In consequence, the Palace as it now stands presents an intriguing mix of architectural styles from pure Thai to Victorian and Italian Renaissance. The Grand Palace comprises five major buildings:

Chakri Maha Prasat lies directly ahead of the main gate, beyond the entrance to the inner courtyard. Built in the reign of Rama V and designed by a British architect, it has an Italianate façade topped by a triple-spired Thai roof. The effect of a contrasting mix of styles is, if strange, generally pleasing.

Dusit Maha Prasat, to the right of Chakri Maha Prasat, was built by Rama I and is a particularly fine example of Thai architecture of the Ratanakosin period. Formerly an audience hall, it is now used for the lying-in-state of kings.

Aphon Phimok Pavilion, next to Dusit Maha Prasat, is an exquisite structure raised to allow the king to transfer from his shoulder-high palanquin to the robing room, where he donned the attire in which he gave audience in the adjacent Throne Hall.

Amarin Winitchai Hall stands to the left of Chakri Maha Prasat. Constructed in Thai style by Rama I, it was formerly the royal court of justice and is now used as the coronation room.

Boromphiman Hall, on the far left, a comparatively modern and uninspiring structure, was built to accommodate state visitors.

Wat Phra Keo (Temple of the Emerald Buddha)

Wat Phra Keo, the most famous and most stunning of Bangkok's more than 400 temples, occupies the northeast corner of the palace compound.

This royal chapel, built by Rama I to enshrine the Emerald Buddha, is quintessential Thailand — a dazzling, colourful Oriental wonder in its collection of pavilions, gilded *chedis*, *prangs* and statuary of strange mythological beings. The blue tiles of the main temple building and the overall splendour of so much rich, decorative detail is indicative of pure Thai religious architecture in which surface decoration is an integral part of the design.

The temple is surrounded by a cloister, the inside walls of which are decorated with murals depicting scenes from the *Ramakien*. These were first painted in the reign of Rama III, but have been restored several times since. In the process they have lost some of their aesthetic purity, though they are still impressive and indicative of the original compositions.

In a line from the entrance to the temple compound are the Phra Sri Ratanna Chedi, the Phra Mondop or library, and the Prasat Phra Thepbidon or royal pantheon, containing statues of the Chakri kings (it is open only once a year, on 6 April, Chakri Day). Next to the Phra Mondop is a model of Angkor Wat constructed at the time when Thailand held sovereignty over Kampuchea.

The statue of the Emerald Buddha is enshrined in the splendid sanctuary in the southern half of the compound (to the right from the entrance). The 75-centimetre (2.4-foot) high image (made of green jasper, not emerald) is raised on a tall, orange pedestal. Its three costumes are worn according to the three seasons and changed by the king at special ceremonies held at the commencement of the hot, rainy and cool seasons.

The origin of the statue is a matter of conjecture and legend. Its recorded history began in 1434 when it was discovered in Chiang Rai after lightning had split open an old *chedi*. It was then covered in plaster and did not attract special attention until that cracked too, revealing the true material beneath. On learning of the mysterious image, the king of Chiang Mai (whose realm included Chiang Rai)

Features of Temple Architecture

Thai temples are magnificent structures, impressive with their soaring multi-tiered roofs and stunning in their rich decorative detail. The *bot* (ordination hall) and *viharn* (hall for daily services), both similar in design, are the biggest and most important buildings, while the following architectural features and details should also be noted:

Chedi — A reliquary tower, synonymous with *stupa*. It is a solid monument, generally but not always tall and of massive proportions, enshrining relics of the Buddha, his disciples, or the ashes of important persons, religious or royal. There are various shapes of *chedis* but the most common is the bell-shape with a tall, tapering spire of graceful proportions. It can have a square base and sometimes, as in the Mon style of Haripunchai, have the form of a stepped pyramid.

Prang — a tall, finger-like spire, usually richly carved. This was a common feature of Khmer religious architecture and was later adopted by Thai builders, typically in the Ayutthaya and Bangkok periods. In Thailand it appears only with the most important religious buildings.

Chofa — Translated as 'sky tassel', this important architectural motif adorns the ridge-ends of the roof of a *bot* or *viharn*. It is a graceful finial in the shape of an elongated bird's head and neck and is commonly held to symbolize the *garuda*. A special ceremony at the conclusion of a temple's construction is held to raise the *chofa*.

Prasat — A tower sanctuary of Khmer origin. The word is sometimes used to refer to the collective structures of a Khmer temple. As adopted by Thai architects, the *prasat* is exclusively a royal or religious edifice, usually of a cruciform pattern and topped by a *prang*. The Golden Meru traditional royal funeral pyre, for example, is in the form of a *prasat*.

Sema — Symbolic foundation stones of a *bot* and the one feature which distinguishes that building from a *viharn*. Placed at the corner and axes on the outside of a *bot*, they are in the form of stone slabs, sometimes decorated with carving.

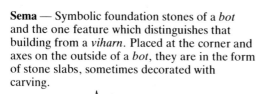

That — Another form of reliquary tower typically found in Laos and the northeast region of Thailand. It has a square base and a tall, tapering tower covered with decorative detail.

Mongkut — An architectural detail comprising tiers of discs rising in gradually diminishing size to a pointed finial. Used to top the *prasat* and other important religious buildings. The tiers represent the 33 levels of Buddhist perfection.

Thai temple architecture employs many varieties of materials usually used in a mosaic of extraordinary complexity to produce an overall stunning effect. Every detail is crafted as though that particular panel, door or fresco was in itself an individual work of art. The two details illustrated here show a section of a gold and black lacquered door and a stone bas relief of Rama which is part of a large frieze depicting the 'Ramakien' epic.

To the left of the visitor's gateway as you enter are four large
chedis (commemorating the first four Chakri kings), numerous smaller
chedis, an old manuscript library, and Chinese- and European-style
pavilions.

In the far left-hand corner of the compound is the large *viharn*
enshrining the enormous Buddha image which gives the temple its
popular name. This is Thailand's largest statue of the Reclining
Buddha and measures 45 metres (145 feet) long and 15 metres (50
feet) high. It is made of brick covered with plaster and gold leaf and is
an impressive sight although, filling virtually the entire interior of the
viharn, it is difficult to appreciate fully its proportions. Most significant
are the soles of the feet which are intricately inlaid with the 108
auspicious signs of the Buddha.

Wat Arun (The Temple of Dawn)

(Open daily) Across the river from Wat Po in Thonburi is Wat Arun,
distinguished by an 86-metre (282-foot) high *prang* raised on a series of
terraces and decorated with embedded pieces of multi-coloured
porcelain which catch the rays of the morning sun. There are four
smaller corner *prangs* and, on the lower terrace, four pavilions each
containing a Buddha image.

The original temple was designated by King Taksin as his royal
chapel when Thonburi was the capital, and until Rama I moved his
base across to Bangkok, it briefly housed the Emerald Buddha.
However, the principal buildings were renovated and the central *prang*
was vastly enlarged during the reigns of Rama II and Rama III.

In 1552 a prince of Chiang Mai removed the statue and took it to
Laos where it remained (first at Luang Prabang and later at Vientiane)
until it was restored to Thailand by General Chakri (later Rama I) in
1778.

Lak Muang

(Open daily) The pavilion enshrining the city pillar or foundation stone
stands across the street from the northeast walls of the Grand Palace
(opposite Wat Phra Keo). Here, covered in gold leaf, is the pillar-like
lingam erected by Rama I as the symbolic foundation of Bangkok as
the capital.

The city's guardian spirit is believed to reside here and the shrine is
popularly held as a source of good fortune, receiving throngs of
supplicants daily. Offerings of thanks are made when wishes are
granted and often take the form of hiring classical dancers to perform.
Thus Lak Muang is one of the best places in Bangkok to see traditional
Thai dance in an authentic setting.

Pramane Ground

Stretching north from the Grand Palace is the open oval space of the royal cremation ground, also referred to as Sanam Lugang (Royal Field). Throughout Bangkok's history it has served as the royal cremation site (last used as such in 1985), but more generally it is the venue for a number of annual celebrations (the Ploughing Ceremony in May, the public gathering on the king's birthday in December), and a recreation area, especially popular for kite-flying from February to April.

Wat Mahathat

(Open daily) Situated on the west side of the Pramane Ground. between Silpakorn and Thammasat Universities, is Wat Mahathat or Temple of the Great Relic. It was built by the Second King (King of the Palace at the Front, a sort of deputy monarch, usually a brother of the king) in the reign of Rama I. Its main buildings comprise two chapels and a *mondop*, although the temple is most important as the national centre for monks of the Mahanikai sect. It is a highly respected hub of Buddhist learning as well as being an important meditation training centre.

Wat Saket and The Golden Mount

(Open daily) Located on the corner of Mahachai Road near its junction with Rajadamnoen Avenue is the 78-metre (256-foot) high artificial hill known as the Golden Mount. Its construction was started by Rama III, who wished to reproduce a similar structure existing in Ayutthaya, but not completed until the reign of Rama V. On the top of the hill, reached by a winding flight of 318 steps, is a gilded *chedi* enshrining sacred relics of the Buddha. There are superb views of the old city area from this vantage point.

At the base of the mount is Wat Saket, dating from the Rama I period and thus one of Bangkok's oldest temples. The *bot* contains murals depicting scenes from the *Ramakien* with registers of praying angels above. In another hall there is a large statue of the standing Buddha, brought from Sukhothai by Rama I. Wat Saket is also famous for its annual temple fair in November, the largest of its kind in Bangkok with food stalls, sideshows and other traditional forms of entertainment.

Wat Rachanada

(Open daily) In the first courtyard of this temple is Bangkok's best-known amulet market, a covered area packed with stalls selling charms which are widely believed to provide the wearer with various forms of protection. Many other religious objects are on sale as well and this is a fascinating place in which to browse.

The temple itself, from the Rama III period, is untypical and comprises a *bot* and two *viharns*. The former's interior is decorated with mural paintings showing scenes of paradise and hell and groups of angels in various parts of the sky. The *viharn* on the left is interesting for its unusual design and the several Ratanakosin-style Buddha images it houses. Behind the main buildings is the curious structure of the Loha Prasat, a pavilion raised on a three-step pyramid and representing a legendary edifice mentioned in the Buddhist chronicles.

Wat Suthat

(Open daily) Located on Bamrung Muang Road, a little way southwest of Wat Rachanada, this temple was built in the first half of the 19th century. It is impressive for the size of its *bot* and *viharn* (the former is probably the tallest in Bangkok). The interiors are no less remarkable, with superb murals and fine collections of Buddha images, including the massive Phra Buddha Chakyamuni which originally came from Sukhothai and is a masterpiece of that period's sculpture.

Giant Swing

Opposite Wat Suthat are the towering twin poles of the Sao Ching Cha, or Giant Swing. Formerly this was the site of a Brahman festival to celebrate the god Siva's annual visit to earth. The highlight of the event involved teams of four young Brahmans, each of whom would swing through a 180° arc to a height of 25 metres (80 feet) above the ground. The object of the exercise was for the man at the prow of the swing to try to grab between his teeth a bag of gold raised on a pole. It was a dangerous business and occasionally performers would fall to their death. The ceremony was officially abolished in 1935.

Wat Rajabophit and Wat Rajapradit

(Open daily) These two temples lie southwest of Wat Suthat between Ban Mo and Sanam Chai Roads. Wat Rajabophit, constructed in 1863, is interesting for its stylistic originality, reflecting Rama V's fascination with Western art and architecture. The Italian Gothic interiors of the two chapels and the relief carvings of soldiers in European-type uniforms at the main entrance reflect these influences. A tall gilded *chedi* with four corner pavilions and a circular cloister distinguish the temple's layout. Rich ornamentation includes pieces of coloured porcelain and mother-of-pearl inlay on doors and windows.

A little way to the west across Klong Lot is Wat Rajapradit, another charming little temple rarely visited by tourists. The main building is raised on a stone platform and is covered in grey marble. There are open-sided corner pavilions and Khmer-style *prangs* on either side, while behind is a *chedi* built by Rama IV.

Wat Bovornivet

(Open daily) Situated on Phra Sumen Road, about a block north of Democracy Monument, Wat Bovornivet is again slightly off the tourist map although well worth visiting. The temple is the headquarters of the Thammayut monastic sect, which follows a stricter discipline than that of the traditional Mahanikai order.

Thammayut was founded by King Mongkut during his 27 years as a monk prior to his succession on the death of Rama III. Mongkut initially retired to Wat Mahathat and then later moved to Wat Bovornivet, where he became abbot and founded the Thammayut order with a desire to return to the original purity of Buddhist teaching. Because of this link with the dynasty, subsequent kings and royal princes have traditionally spent their time of monastic retreat at Wat Bovornivet.

The Dusit Area

What might be termed the new royal city lies to the northeast of Bangkok's historic heart in Dusit, an area largely developed by King Chulalongkorn, Rama V. This district is characterised by comparatively wide, tree-lined streets.

The main approach is via the broad Rajadamnoen Nok Avenue which leads into the square in front of the old National Assembly, a building of Italianate design. It was constructed in 1907 as Chulalongkorn's Throne Hall. With the advent of the democratic system after the revolution of 1932, it became the National Assembly until new premises were provided in 1974. The building is not commonly open to the public.

In the centre of the square is an equestrian statue of King Chulalongkorn, while to the left are Amporn Gardens, an attractive park frequently the venue for royal-sponsored social functions and fairs.

which stands in extensive grounds and is mostly obscured from public gaze. It was constructed by Rama VI and adopted as the royal residence by the present king.

Wat Benchamabopit

(Open daily) This is the most famous sight in the Dusit area, located on Sri Ayutthaya Road between Chitralada Palace and the old National Assembly. Built by Rama V, it is the newest of Bangkok's royal temples, and is constructed largely from Carrara marble, hence the popular name 'Marble Temple'.

The *bot*, distinguished by its three-tiered roof of yellow Chinese tile and portico entrance with flanking statues of mythical lions, is an impressive sight, and the overall design of the temple, the work of Prince Naris, half brother to Chulalongkorn and accomplished man of the arts, is extremely pleasing.

Wat Benchamabopit is also famous for its courtyard gallery which houses more than 50 Buddha images (many are reproductions of important statues), illustrating styles from all periods of Thai Buddhist art and from other Buddhist countries. The presiding Buddha statue in the *bot* is a copy of the highly revered Phra Buddha Chinaraj, the original of which is at Wat Phra Sri Mahathat in Phitsanulok.

Dusit Zoo

(Open daily 8 am−6 pm, admission ฿10, children half price) Correctly named Khao Din (Mountain of Earth) Zoo because of the man-made hill which dominates the topography, this is one of the best zoos in Southeast Asia.

Vimanmek Throne Hall

(Open Wednesday to Friday 9.30 am−4 pm, admission ฿50) Recently opened to the public as the private museum of Rama V, the four-storey wooden building behind the National Assembly opposite Dusit Zoo houses a collection of antique furniture, paintings and jewellery belonging to Thai royalty.

Chinatown

When Bangkok was designated as the capital, the Chinese traders who had occupied the banks of the river were moved downstream to make way for the Grand Palace. They resettled in the area known as Sampeng, which is still the city's Chinatown. The district is close to the southern curve of the Chao Phraya's broad loop and is traversed by

Charoen Krung (New) Road and Yaowaraj Road.

The area is characterized by narrow streets jam-packed with shops and stalls offering an exotic mix of merchandise. The whole area is pervaded by a frenetic air of commercial activity. Gold shops, always painted red and white and making much use of mirror glass, are Chinatown's most famous retailers, but you will also find many goods that may be described as ethnic — traditional medicines made from tiger bone, snake wine and other ingredients unheard of in the Western pharmacopoeia; colourful paper models of houses, cars, refrigerators and other symbols of material success which are burnt at funerals to ensure the deceased every comfort in the hereafter.

The most typical of the district's streets, Sampeng Lane (Soi Wanit), a long, narrow pedestrian way, is packed with all sorts of stalls. At its northern end is Pahurat Cloth Market, popularly called the Indian Market, with a contrasting mix of ethnic goods, notably fabrics.

Also in Chinatown between Charoen Krung and Yaowaraj roads is **Thieves Market**, Nakhon Kasem. No longer the 'fence's' showcase that gave rise to its popular name, the market offers a mix of modern goods and antiques-cum-*objets d'art*. Brassware is abundant and other good buys include gongs, chests, cabinets and other old furniture, Chinese porcelain and snuff bottles. Bargaining is *de rigueur*.

There are a few Chinese temples tucked away in Chinatown, the most important of which is **Wat Leng Noi Yi** on Charoen Krung. At one time Bangkok's leading Chinese temple, it has a fascinating collection of statues and images, of various Chinese deities and of the Buddha, while in the compound are workshops turning out paper funeral offerings.

At the southern end of Charoen Krung and Yaowaraj Roads, near Hualampong Railway Station, just before Chinatown begins, is **Wat Traimit**, Temple of the Golden Buddha. The Golden Buddha statue was rediscovered some 40 years ago when what was apparently a stucco Buddha was being removed from a ruined temple. The statue fell from the crane lifting it and the plaster cracked revealing the precious metal beneath. Fashioned in the Sukhothai style, it was probably coated with stucco to hide it from the Burmese when they invaded Ayutthaya in the 18th century.

Modern Bangkok

The districts in the southern and eastern parts of the city, referred to by their main thoroughfares, Silom and Sukhumvit respectively, comprise what might be termed modern Bangkok. Here and close by are to be found most of the major tourist hotels, along with the principal shopping, entertainment and commercial centres.

Old Farang Quarter

The stretch of Charoen Krung (New) Road at the river end of Silom Road is the site of Bangkok's old European quarter which blossomed in the late 19th and early 20th centuries. Reminders of this period are to be found in the Oriental Hotel (still the city's best and retaining one small original wing); the colonial-style offices of the East Asiatic Company, doyen of the early foreign trading concerns; Oriental Plaza, again a colonial-style building now converted as an up-market shopping centre; Assumption Cathedral, Bangkok's principal Catholic church; the French and Portuguese embassies; and, next to the Royal Orchid Sheraton Hotel, the modern River City Shopping Complex.

A little further south on New Road, between the Silom and Sathorn intersections, is **Bangrak Market**, one of Bangkok's main fresh produce outlets. It is a traditional covered market, its outside thronged by cut-flower sellers (very cheap orchids).

Lumpini Park facing Rama IV Road opposite the Silom intersection, is the city's principal patch of greenery. The park has a lake with small paddle boats for hire. It is also the place to come early in the morning to jog or watch people practising Tai Ji Quan (Tai Chi), the ancient Chinese system of exercise and self-defence carried out in a kind of slow-motion, shadow-boxing action.

Snake Farm

(Open daily 8.30 am–4 pm, admission ฿10) Also on Rama IV Road near Lumpini Park is the Snake Farm at the Pasteur Institute which produces antidote for snake bites. It houses a large collection of cobras and other venomous snakes, which are milked daily at 11 am.

Erawan Shrine

(Open daily) On the way towards the Sukhumvit area, on the corner of Ploenchit and Rajdamri Roads, next to the Hyatt Hotel, is the Erawan Shrine. Here a small pavilion enshrines a statue of Brahma, the four-headed Hindu god. It was originally constructed during the building of the hotel to ward off bad luck, but now it has become Bangkok's most famous source of good fortune. The tiny area is packed daily with supplicants making wishes or giving traditional offerings of thanks—flower garlands, incense, food, wooden model elephants (the elephant Erawan is the mythical mount of Brahma). Classical dancers also perform here—a curious and fascinating sight made more startling by its location at one of Bangkok's busiest traffic intersections.

Museums and Gardens

National Museum

(Open daily except Monday and Friday 9 am—noon and 1—4 pm, admission ฿20, free on Sunday) Located opposite the northwest corner of the Pramane Ground, the National Museum houses a fine collection of Thai sculpture from all periods, along with ethnological exhibits and examples of the performing arts, most notably marionettes and shadow theatre.

As it occupies part of the old Palace of the Front (built in 1782) it boasts a number of buildings that can be considered exhibits in their own right. Finest among these is the Phutthaisawan Chapel, one of the best examples of monastic architecture of the early Bangkok period. Constructed in 1787 to house the greatly revered Buddha image of Phra Buddhasihing, its walls are decorated with murals depicting scenes from the life of the Buddha.

Other buildings of note in the museum compound include the residential quarters of King Pin Klao, Second King of Rama IV; the Isarawinitchai Hall, formerly the audience hall of the Palace of the Front; the Manghalaphisak pavilion; and the Tamnak Deang or Red House, a splendid wooden structure dating from the reign of Rama I but not originally part of the Palace of the Front.

Jim Thompson's House

(Open Monday to Friday 9 am—4 pm, admission ฿50) Located at the end of Soi Kasemsan 2 across from the National Stadium on Rama I Road is the traditional Thai house reconstructed by Jim Thompson. This remarkable American settled in Bangkok after World War II and went into business to revitalize the local silk industry. In this he was eminently successful and Jim Thompson silk is still one of Bangkok's top buys at the shop he opened at No. 9 Suriwong Road. Thompson achieved legendary status when he disappeared without a trace while on holiday in Malaysia in 1967—one of the East's greatest modern mysteries.

Besides having a great interest in silk, Thompson was a great lover of Thai art and antiquities. His house, which is now a museum, is a brilliant example of traditional domestic architecture and was reconstructed by him from six old houses to form an appropriate setting for his beautiful collection of antiques. The house, with its typical *klong*-side location, is an attraction in its own right, while the collection of stone and bronze sculpture, porcelain, woodcarving and paintings is priceless.

Suan Pakkard Palace

(Open daily except Sunday 9 am—4 pm, admission ฿50) Here, on Si Ayutthaya Road, is a superb collection of traditional Thai houses set amid extensive landscaped gardens. Belonging to one of Thailand's leading patrons of the arts, the complex offers fine old-style architecture, a rare lacquer pavilion (a masterpiece of decorative art), an excellent collection of bronze and stone art works, ceramics and furniture, in addition to the gardens.

Hilton International Hotel

The hotel, on Wireless Road, has perhaps the best landscaped tropical gardens in Bangkok, with a large variety of flowering shrubs and trees. In one corner is the curious shrine dedicated to the female spirit of Chao Mae Tuptim. Considerably pre-dating the hotel, it is, like the Erawan Shrine, popularly believed to be a source of divine assistance. Its peculiarity is that offerings of thanks traditionally take the form of phallic symbols, hundreds of which in all sizes surround the shrine.

Kamthieng House

(Open Tuesday to Saturday 9 am—noon and 1—5 pm, admission ฿25) Located in the compound of the Siam Society (a royal-sponsored association for the promotion of Thai studies) on Soi Asoke (Soi 21), Sukhumvit Road, this old house is a fine example of traditional northern architecture. It was formerly the home of a prominent family in Chiang Mai until it was donated to the Society. After being dismantled and brought down from the north, it was reconstructed on the present site. Inside is a collection of ethnological artifacts relating to the people and culture of northern Thailand.

Markets

Besides Bangrak and Thieves markets there are a number of old-style retail outlets scattered around the city.

Weekend Market (Open Saturday and Sunday), at Chatuchak Park, off Phaholyothin Road and near the Northern Bus Terminal, is Bangkok's most glorious all-purpose market. A staggering array of open-air stalls spread out over a huge area peddle a spectrum of merchandise from fruit, vegetables and household goods to fabrics, new and secondhand clothing, shoes, toys and tape cassettes to handicrafts, antiques, potted plants, pets of various species and army surplus goods.

Pratunam Market, which spans both sides of Ratchaprarop Road

Taming the Dragon

While lying on the river at Petchaburee, an inland city about seventy-five miles from Bangkok, I was awakened by the most hideous noise; the firing of guns, shooting of crackers, beating of drums and tom-toms and the shouting of a vast multitude. Looking out of the window of my boat a weird spectacle presented itself to my vision. The whole place was lighted up by huge bonfires on the banks of the stream and the air full of glittering rockets. Calling my kavass I inquired what was the occasion of the hubbub? Touching the points of his fingers together and raising them up on a level with his breast, he replied, "Your Excellency, the great dragon has the moon swallowed up." Having heard that the natives thus celebrated the approach of an eclipse, I stepped ashore and mingled with the crowd which was made up of all classes, old and young, with a large sprinkling of yellow-robed priests who were as active as the others in keeping up the unearthly din. It was a lovely morn, the southern cross hung like a gleaming jewel in the upper deep, gentle zephyrs perfumed by myriads of flowers fanned the brow and waved the feathery bamboo as gently as the coquette her fan, the round orbed moon, a bright silver disk, was suspended in the western heavens, burnished like the shield of Achilles, while all around burned the many fires which shed a glare on the crowd of half-clad adults and naked children. A shadow had just fallen upon the surface of the queen of night, slowly it spread over it until the face of the great luminary was covered, and it hung in the cloudless heavens an orb of roseate hue, its radiance all gone. Then the noise became terrific, the reports of guns and crackers were almost deafening, which increased as a gleam of silver tinged the outer rim of the dimmed goddess. Slowly the shadow passed away, the light growing brighter and brighter, the great dragon Asura Rahu, that had attempted to swallow the moon, had been driven away and it again shone in all of its brilliancy, but soon faded away before the corruscations of the coming dawn. It was a scene worthy of the pen of an Arnold or the pencil of a Titian: the ruddy glow of the flowing water, the multitude upon the river banks with its white houses embowered in dense foliage, the frantic efforts of the people as the shadow drifted across the disk of the moon and fell across the landscape and the glare of the fires that lighted up the immediate surroundings, a spectacle that could be witnessed nowhere else save in the interior of Siam, where no white man dwells and the native clings to his superstitions as religiously as did his forefathers ere the present dynasty ascended the throne of this kingdom. It was early morn ere peace reigned once more, and when the sun rose amid the pearliest of skies its beams lit up a lovely scene, gilding the spires of the wats and roofs of the palaces; business had resumed its sway, the fisherman was hawking fish, the fruitier his fruit, the merchant had displayed his goods on the counter, the priests were gathering their food into their rice pots for the day's provender and the moon and the dragon seemed to have passed into oblivion, the only evidence of the nocturnal saturnalia being the smoking pyres that had been lighted and the exploded red and white crackers that strewed the ground.

Jacob T Child, The Pearl of Asia (1892)

by its intersection with Petchaburi Road, specializes in fresh produce, clothing, fabrics and haberdashery.

Tewes Market, at the river end of Krung Kasem Road near the National Library, is the best place for flowers and potted plants.

Pak Klong Market, at the foot of Memorial Bridge on the Bangkok side, is the city's wholesale centre for fruit, vegetables and cut flowers.

Sanam Luang Bookstalls, on the corner of Rajadamnoen Avenue facing Sanam Luang, is the traditional spot for students to pick up secondhand textbooks. It also has a large selection of foreign language paperbacks and magazines.

Thonburi

Wat Arun is the most famous monument on the Thonburi side of the Chao Phraya River, but the less renowned temples in the area are also worth visiting.

Wat Kalayanimit, near the mouth of Klong Bangkok Yai, is easily reached by the cross-river ferry from the Tha Rachini landing stage next to Pak Klong Market. This temple, built in the reign of Rama III, is distinguished by its main *viharn* of unusually tall proportions, an architectural feature dictated by the huge statue of the Buddha inside. Wat Kalayanimit is also fascinating for its compound and monks' quarters which, in their riverine setting, give one a sense of how old Bangkok must have looked.

Wat Prayoon, a little way downstream from Wat Kalayanimit, beyond Santa Cruz Church, is most noted for the small artificial hill to the right of the entrance. It is a charming spot dotted with *chedis* and frangipani trees and surrounded by a pond full of turtles. It was created, so the story goes, after King Rama III noticed one night how the melted wax from his candle formed a curiously shaped mount. He remarked on this to a courtier who later had the hill constructed after the wax model.

Wat Suwannaram and Wat Dusitaram, located further upstream near the junction with Klong Bangkok Noi, both have foundations dating from the Ayutthaya period but were reconstructed by King Rama I. The former is an especially good example of the architectural style that bridges the Ayutthaya and Rattanakosin (Bangkok) eras. More striking, however, are the interiors which are decorated with late 18th- and early 19th-century mural paintings of exceptional quality.

Nearby on Klong Bangkok Noi is the shed housing a collection of highly ornate **royal barges**, formerly used on state ceremonial occasions but today rarely seen (the last occasion was during the 1982 Rattanakosin Bicentennial). Open daily 8.30 am—4.30 pm, admission ฿10.

Waterways and Floating Markets

Most of the *klongs* (canals) on the Bangkok side of the river have been filled in to make way for roads, but in Thonburi many of the old waterways are still in use, and you can cruise along the back canals by hiring your own longtail boat (*hang yao*) from one of the landing stages on the Bangkok side. (Oriental Pier next to the Oriental Hotel is popular for this, though prices are likely to be higher; try instead the Tha Rachini landing stage near Memorial Bridge. Bargaining is the rule and a reasonable rate for a longtail boat is ฿150−300 per hour. One boat can comfortably take six to eight people.)

For longer river trips, the *Oriental Queen*, operated by the Oriental Hotel, runs daily cruises upriver to Ayutthaya and an evening dinner cruise every Wednesday. Tours on this luxury air-conditioned river cruiser can be booked through leading tour agents or at the Oriental.

Alternatively, full-day excursions by public boat to the **Stork Sanctuary** (nesting season is October to April) at Wat Pailom in Pathum Thani, or to Wat Pailongwua in Suphanburi (noted for the weird statuary in its 'Buddhist Park') are operated on Sundays and public holidays, departing between 7 and 8 am from Tha Tien and Tha Maharaj landing stages. Fares are inexpensive. For further details call Chao Phraya Express Boat Co Ltd, tel. 411-0418, or Sukserm Express Boat Service, tel. 211-2296.

The **Floating Market** (commerce carried out from small sampans) in Thonburi has been over-exposed to tourism and has suffered accordingly. Much more authentic and bigger is the Floating Market at Damnoen Saduak, west of Bangkok. Regular tours are operated daily by leading travel agents. It should be visited in the early morning.

Shopping

Since Bangkok lacks any one obvious downtown area, shopping districts are scattered throughout the city. The following three areas, however, can be recommended for the volume, variety and quality of their shops: **Silom-Suriwong-New Road**, which includes Robinson and Central department stores on Silom Road, and Oriental Plaza (up-market antiques, art objects and handicrafts) and River City Shopping Complex (fourth floor devoted to antique stores) both off New Road; **Rajdamri-Ploenchit-Gaysorn** boasting the largest concentration of department stores in this area; and **Rama I Road-Siam Square-Siam Centre**.

The shopping arcades of most first-class hotels are good if you are short of time, but of course prices tend to be higher.

Most shops are open six days a week, while several (including

Thai Boxing

Thai boxing (*muay-thai*) is the national pastime of Thailand. At first glance it seems to be a rather violent and vulgar affair. The spectators, almost exclusively male, are loud, vociferous, and apparently as much aficionados of the art of gambling as of *muay-thai* itself. Yet, like much in Thai society, a closer, more careful look reveals layers of culture, tradition and even aesthetic beauty that make Thai boxing more than merely thrilling entertainment.

As you jostle your way up to the ticket window through the teeming multitude of fans and vendors, you begin to sense the excitement and the unvarying intensity of the fans' passion for their national sport. After making your way in and finding a seat (second-class seats are the best for watching the action both in the ring and the stands; third-class is for inveterate gamblers and anthropologists; ringside is for the rich and famous), note the orchestra, seated on a platform to one side of the ring. Composed of traditional Thai instruments, it is an integral part of the ritual to follow.

The first two fighters enter the arena, followed by their trainers and handlers. Like their Western counterparts, they are wearing robes, boxing shorts, and 12- or 16-ounce boxing gloves. But the similarities end there. These boxers are barefoot and wear an armband (the *khruang-rang*) around their biceps, with an amulet tied or sewn in. Also, during the pre-game ritual they wear a strange-looking headband (the *mong-khon*), which is a hallowed talisman bestowed upon them by their trainers.

The orchestra begins playing at a slow, steady cadence as the boxers begin their 'boxing dance' (*ram-muay*). It starts with a show of respect to the teacher (*wai-khroo*), kneeling and bowing three times. The dance that follows is a combination of religious ritual (driving away evil spirits) and intimidation. The *ram-muay* is very difficult to master, and a boxer's display of proficiency in the dance will earn a fighter not only murmurs of admiration from connoisseurs in the audience, but respect for his fighting skills from his opponent as well.

During the fight which follows you will see the combatants exchange vicious blows to head and body using feet, fists, knees, elbows — in fact with virtually every potential weapon of the body except the head (butting is prohibited, as in Western-style boxing). The tempo and intensity of the music rises and falls with the level of intensity in the ring. All this clamour and fury may seem light-years removed from the spirituality and aesthetics of the *ram-muay*. Yet the paradox is explained if we look at the history of the sport.

Like the Chinese, Okinawan and Japanese martial arts, *muay-thai* began as a combination of self-defence and hand-to-hand combat techniques practised by warriors for use in battle. Over time, these techniques were refined and formalized by martial arts masters, who strung the best movements together into a kind of stylized dance, thus preserving and systematizing their teaching. The *ram-muay* is just such a series of fighting movements, a link to both the spiritual and martial traditions of the ancient Thai. And while boxing is a decidedly professional occupation — every fight is a prize fight — the concentration and discipline needed to master the pain and fear could not be attained without the devotional and spiritual training represented by the *wai-khroo* and the *ram-muay*.

The best place to see a *muay-thai* match in Bangkok is Lumpini Stadium, on Rama IV Road. Matches are held Tuesdays, Fridays and Saturdays beginning at 6 pm. Lumpini is a funky, old wooden structure, smaller and more intimate than the other, more modern 'Grand Palace' of Thai boxing, Rajadamnoen Stadium (matches Mondays, Wednesdays and Thursdays at 6 pm, Sundays at 5 pm).

Seats cost upwards of ฿100.

department stores) are also open on Sundays and public holidays. Hours are usually 9 am−6.30 pm, although smaller establishments tend to open earlier and close later.

Nightlife

Such is the city's reputation that to say 'Bangkok by night' conjures up images of unbridled sex in most people's minds. The reputation is not ill-founded and Bangkok has a disproportionate number of nightclubs, go-go bars and massage parlours with an estimated 300,000 hostesses, bar girls and masseuses. And that is not to mention the gay scene.

It should be pointed out, however, that there is little pathos or seediness surrounding such attractions, certainly nothing to compare with the gross nature of red-light districts in Western cities. In keeping with the Thai character, the idea of *sanuk*, having a good time, predominates, and whatever anyone does is his or her business with no harm to anyone else.

The main go-go bar areas are Patpong I and Patpong II, two small streets running between Silom and Suriwong Roads, and Soi Cowboy, a narrow lane between Sois 21 and 23 off Sukhumvit Road.

Massage parlours (open 5 pm−midnight on weekdays and 2 pm−midnight on weekends and public holidays) are found throughout the city with concentrations in Patpong and on New Petchaburi Road.

While such nightlife attractions are primarily oriented towards the single male, it is not uncommon for female visitors to go to a bar or massage parlour; there are certainly no restrictions.

Evening entertainment is not limited to the salacious, however. Performances of classical dance and cultural shows are put on at a number of restaurants specializing in Thai cuisine. Most top hotels have cocktail lounges with live music, and several also have discotheques. If the latter is your scene, however, the 'in' place is The Palace on Vibhavadi Rangist Road (the highway leading to the airport). It is big, noisy and crowded, and caters most decidedly to the young set.

Movie theatres abound though the number of foreign films (with original soundtrack) is rather limited due to high import duties.

A typically local form of evening entertainment is Thai boxing in which feet, legs, knees and elbows are used in addition to gloved fists (see page 90).

Around Bangkok

The following places can all be covered comfortably on day excursions from Bangkok, either by public transport or, in most cases, by organized tours operated daily by leading travel agents (usually bookable through hotel travel counters).

North

Ayutthaya

The Thai capital from 1350 to 1767, Ayutthaya is the most important historical site within easy striking distance of Bangkok. Situated on the Chao Phraya River, 85 kilometres (53 miles) from Bangkok, it can be reached by bus, train or, most luxuriously, by the air-conditioned river cruiser *Oriental Queen* which departs daily at 8 am from the Oriental Hotel (the full day tour is one way by boat and one way by tour bus).

Although sacked, looted and razed by Burmese invaders in the 18th century, the surviving ruins of Ayutthaya (the major monuments have been restored as far as possible) stand as testament to the former glory of what was once the most magnificent city in the Orient (see pages 15–17).

Ayutthaya is an island city on the Chao Phraya River at its junction with the Pa Sak and Lopburi tributaries, linked by a canal to bring the water all around. The riverine setting survives to this day and an initial exploration around the waterways of the city can be made by hiring a boat from the landing stage near Chandra Kasem Palace in the northeast corner of town.

Sights

The ruins are scattered around the modern town. Its more illustrious forerunner was once surrounded by a 12-kilometre (seven-mile) enclosing wall and boasted three major palace complexes and some 400 temples. There were separate quarters, or trading factories, supporting sizeable communities of foreign residents both occidental and oriental.

Ayutthaya was not only the physical power centre of the nation, it symbolized the whole concept of nationhood and protected the religious and cultural traditions of the Thai people. During its 417-year history it was the capital for 33 kings of five dynasties.

Wat Phra Sri Sanphet This was the royal temple and originally stood within the compound of the king's palace. (The latter, comprising seven buildings, was destroyed by the Burmese and only scattered foundations remain to give an inkling of its original extent.) Wat Phra Sri Sanphet, built in 1448 and renovated at least twice, formerly housed a 16-metre (50-foot) Buddha image covered in gold leaf which gave the temple its name. The statue was ruined in the Burmese attack and today the temple is distinguished by its row of three *chedis* typical of the Ayutthaya style.

Viharn Phra Mongkol Bopit Close to Wat Phra Sri Sanphet, this modern building dating from the 1950s enshrines the enormous bronze Buddha statue of Phra Mongkol Bopit, one of the largest in Thailand.

Wat Phra Ram This temple, a little way southeast of Wat Phra Sri Sanphet, was first constructed in 1369 by King Ramesuan, the second monarch of Ayutthaya, on the site where the remains of King U

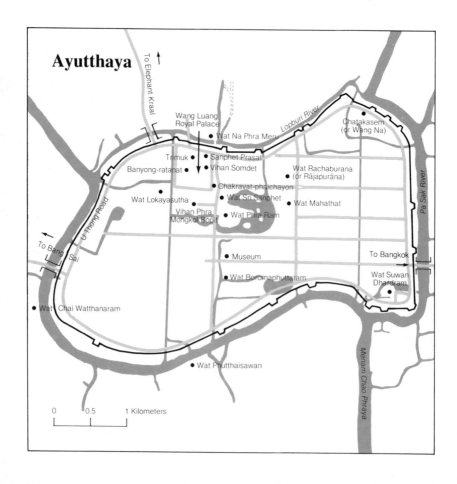

Thong, his father, were cremated. It was twice entirely renovated. The ruins are dominated by a large central *prang*.

Wat Mahathat On the eastern side of the lake opposite Wat Phra Ram stand the extensive ruins of Wat Mahathat. The buildings date from the 14th century and have been severely damaged although the *prang*, now less than half its original height, is still impressive.

Wat Rachaburana Situated across the road from Wat Mahathat, this was similarly a large temple complex and is in a better state of preservation with a particularly fine *prang*. It was built in 1424 by King Borommaracha II to commemorate his two elder brothers whose ashes are housed in twin *chedis* still to be seen.

Wat Yanasen and Wat Thammikarat The ruins of these two temples lie west of Wat Rachaburana. The former is noted for its *chedi* which, not having suffered from unsatisfactory restoration, is an especially good example of Ayutthaya workmanship. The ruins of Wat Thammikarat are also interesting and have an added attraction in their air of romantic charm.

Wat Na Phra Meru (Phra Mane) Located across the river north of the site of the Royal Palace is this restored temple. In its *viharn* is a Dvaravati stone Buddha image seated European fashion with hands on knees, while its *bot* enshrines a good Ayutthaya-style bronze seated Buddha.

Wat Suwan Dhararam Located in the southeast corner of Ayutthaya, this temple was built by the father of King Rama I shortly before the fall of the city. Renovated twice (by Rama I and Rama III), it is in excellent condition and is still used. The *bot* has the typical Ayutthaya architectural feature of concave foundations, so that the side walls dip in the middle, and the interior walls are decorated with mural paintings.

Wat Yai Chai Mongkol and Wat Phanan Choeng These two monuments also lie to the southeast but on the opposite side of the river. The former is distinguished by a high *chedi* constructed to commemorate King Naresuan's victory in single-handed, elephant-back combat over the crown prince of Burma in 1592. Wat Phanan Choeng, close to the river bank, is notable in that it is believed to pre-date the founding of Ayutthaya as the capital by some 26 years. It enshrines a massive image of the seated Buddha.

Phu Khao Thong (Golden Mount Chedi) This monument lies two kilometres (1.25 miles) outside the city to the northwest and rises imposingly to dominate the surrounding flat countryside. The soaring *chedi* raised on terraces was originally built in Mon style by the Burmese after their first conquest of Ayutthaya in 1569, but the present structure was rebuilt in Thai style by King Borommakot in 1745.

Museums There are two museums in Ayutthaya, the main one being the Chao Sam Phraya Museum in the centre of town on Rojana Road (open Wednesday to Sunday 9 am—noon and 1 pm—4 pm, admission ฿5). It houses a fine collection of bronze, stone and terracotta statues, mostly from the Ayutthaya period but with some representatives of the Lopburi and U Thong styles, and affords a good introduction to the art of Ayutthaya.

The other, smaller museum is at Chan Kasem Palace in the northeast corner of the city (opening times as above). The building, a museum piece in its own right, stands on the site of the palace where King Naresuan lived before he was crowned, and was reconstructed in the 19th century by King Mongkut. It occupies a pleasant compound with gardens, a tranquil oasis compared to the busy street outside.

Bang Pa-In

On the Chao Phraya River a few kilometres downstream from Ayutthaya is the former royal summer retreat of Bang Pa-In (open daily except Monday, 8.30 am—noon and 1 pm—4 pm, admission ฿10). The palace comprises a collection of buildings in a surprising variety of architectural styles — Thai, Chinese, Italian, Victorian — which, enhanced by the grounds and ornamental ponds, possess a certain picture-postcard charm.

Bang Pa-In was first used by the kings of Ayutthaya in the 17th century, although it fell into disuse after the Burmese invasion of 1767 and the buildings seen today date from the late 19th and early 20th centuries.

The palace no longer serves as a royal retreat during the hot season and is rarely used. Nevertheless, the only building open to the public is the ornate Chinese-style Vehat Chamroon Palace. This and the Thai-style Aisawan Tippaya Asna pavilion, enchantingly raised over a pond, are the two most striking buildings in the complex.

Bang Pa-In can be reached by bus, car or, most pleasantly, by boat from Ayutthaya. It is also included in the *Oriental Queen*'s Ayutthaya cruise.

Lopburi

This historically important town north of Ayutthaya on the Lopburi River 153 kilometres (95 miles) from Bangkok is not yet well-established on the tourist itinerary but is a must for anyone interested in 17th-century Thai history.

Originally called Louvo, it was already an important town during the Dvaravati and Khmer periods. It reached its zenith during the reign of King Narai (1656−88) who made it the 'second city' of Ayutthaya and used it for all intents and purposes as the kingdom's capital. It was here that the king's chief minister, Constance Phaulkon (see page 19), built his residence, close to Narai's palace where the French embassy headed by Chevalier de Chaumont was received in 1685.

After the palace revolution of 1688, led by Phra Phetracha, Phaulkon was executed on charges (arguably trumped up) of treason. After taking the throne, Phetracha re-established royal residence at Ayutthaya and Lopburi fell into decline.

Sights

Today the town is a provincial capital and a sizeable army base; its modern appearance is not inspiring. Nevertheless, scattered among the latter-day development are some excellent ruins attesting to the rich and eventful past. The major sights are listed below in historical order.

Phra Prang Sam Yot Located in the centre of the old town on a grassy mound next to the railway crossing is the classic monument to Lopburi's Khmer heritage. Built in the 13th century, it comprises three *prangs* linked by a central corridor and is a well-preserved example of Khmer architecture indicative of the Bayon style. The huge laterite blocks were once covered with stucco and a few traces of this decoration can still be seen. Originally constructed as a Hindu shrine, Phra Prang Sam Yot was later used as a Buddhist temple and two of the towers contain partially-ruined Buddha statues in the Lopburi style. In front to the east is a brick *viharn* probably built in the reign of King Narai.

Prang Khaek Situated in a square in the middle of town this is another Khmer relic, a Hindu sanctuary comprising the fairly well-preserved ruins of a central tallish tower and two smaller flanking *prangs*. Made of brick, it has been restored, although stylistic influences suggesting the Angkor period indicate it could have been first constructed in the tenth century.

Wat Phra Si Ratana Mahathat (Open daily 8.30 am−4 pm, admission ฿20) Lopburi's most impressive and important religious ruin is to be found in the southern part of town opposite the railway station. The trip to Lopburi is rewarding for this monument alone.

The origins of the temple complex, which covers an area of three hectares (7.4 acres), are unknown although it is certain that it spans the Khmer period and Narai's reign. The ruins are dominated by a large laterite Khmer *prang* which was probably first constructed in the 12th century. The superb structure shows Bayon influences in the surviving traces of stucco decoration, but its design is untypical and so

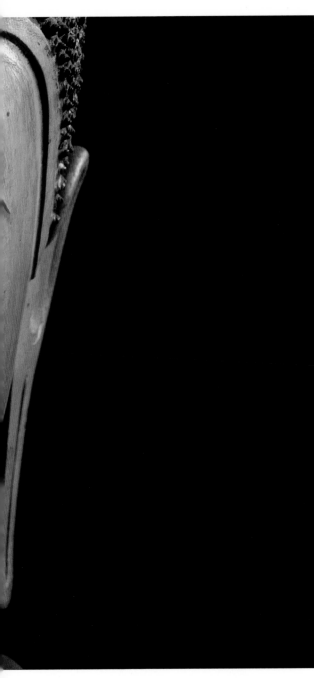

This gilded bronze Buddha image represents what many believe to be the apex of Thai religious art. Of the middle U Thong period dating from the 14th century, this golden age of Thai art history spanned both the Sukhothai and Ayutthaya historical periods. This piece is now in the private collection of Praku Knanumsommanajara.

it is thought the building seen today dates from the time when the Thais were beginning to overshadow the Khmer in the region.

The other principal feature, the large brick *viharn*, was clearly built in the reign of King Narai and displays Western and Persian styles in its pointed arch windows.

Dotting the site are a number of *chedis* and *prangs*, as well as remains of cloisters and of enclosing walls.

Phra Narai Rajanivet (The Palace of King Narai — open Wednesday to Sunday 9 am—noon and 1—4 pm, admission ฿20) The huge battlements of the palace built by King Narai between 1665 and 1677 dominate the western side of town close to the banks of the Lopburi River. The main entrance is via the Pratu (gate) Phayakkha on Sorasak Road. The latter is presumably named after Luang Sorasak, son of Phra Phetracha, who hated Phaulkon and, when Narai was dying, set a trap and captured the Greek as he was entering the palace via this gate. Phaulkon was then imprisoned and tortured for a few days until one night he was led out of the palace on elephant back and taken to his place of execution.

Partially designed by French architects, the palace buildings were laid out in three compounds, formerly separated by inner walls. The first area was devoted to government buildings, the second to ceremonial buildings and the inner compound to Narai's private residence. An interesting feature on the inside of some of the walls are the rows of niches that would have contained oil lamps on ceremonial occasions, doubtless creating an impressive sight.

After the death of Narai, Phetracha remained in Lopburi only long enough for his coronation and then abandoned the place in favour of Ayutthaya. The palace fell into disrepair until the 19th century when King Mongkut restored part of it and added his own pavilion (in a mix of Thai, Chinese and European styles).

Today most of the 17th-century buildings are completely ruined, although the palace grounds are well-tended and maintained as a kind of public park.

In the first courtyard as you enter there are on the left the remains of storehouses and a reservoir and, at the far end, what survives of the elephant stables. In the adjacent quadrangle to the left are the ruins of the reception hall and the Phra Chao Hao building, which may have once enshrined an important Buddha image.

Further inside, in the northwest quadrangle are traces of the Suttha Sawan pavilion where Narai died. In the heart of the palace, next to Mongkut's pavilion, is the Chanthara Phisan, constructed by Narai and restored in the 19th century. Behind these two buildings was the closed-in royal harem. Left of Mongkut's pavilion (as you face it) are the ruins of the Dusit Sawan Thanya Maha Prasat, formerly used for receiving foreign ambassadors and where de Chaumont delivered the famous letter from King Louis XIV in 1685 during his audience with Narai.

The pavilion built by King Mongkut now serves as a museum and contains a small but fine collection of Lopburi-style sculpture and other artifacts.

Wat Sao Thong Thong Situated directly north of Narai's palace, this temple is noted for its *viharn* which was originally a Christian chapel during the Narai period and later converted to Buddhist use. The other old buildings in the compound also date from the Narai period and were once used as residences by the ambassadors from Persia.

Phaulkon's House (Open daily 8.30 am−4 pm, admission ฿20) The residence built by Constance Phaulkon, or Chao Phraya Wichayen (the title conferred by King Narai), stands across the street from Wat Sao Thong Thong. Within the walled compound can be seen the fairly substantial ruins of three main buildings: on the west Phaulkon's house itself, in the centre a Catholic church and residence of the Jesuits and, on the east side, the accommodation constructed for members of the 1685 French mission. The brick and cement edifices are an odd blend of architectural styles in which European predominates, but not to the total exclusion of Thai influences.

Wat Tong Pou This 400-year-old temple, located off the street which cuts through the northeast corner of the old town, is less well-known than the other sights of Lopburi and is undeservedly neglected by visitors. To be seen are a venerable *bot*, with a two-tier tiled roof, an equally old *viharn*, a small library and a little bell tower with some stucco decoration. The *bot* and the *viharn* contain a number of Buddha images, most in the Lopburi style, and the compound is dotted with several old small *chedis*.

Northeast

Wang Takrai Park

This park is the perfect destination for a day trip into the countryside. It is best covered by hiring your own car and driver in Bangkok.

Encompassing 80 hectares (200 acres), Wang Takrai was created in 1955 by the late Prince Chumbot of Nagara Svarga and subsequently opened to the public by his widow who has continued to develop the landscaped gardens. Situated in a picturesque valley 106 kilometres (66 miles) from Bangkok, the park is traversed by a stream and is planted with a large variety of trees, shrubs and flowers.

Master of the House

Such was Chow Phya Sri Sury Wongse when I was first presented to him: a natural king among the dusky forms that surrounded him, the actual ruler of that semi-barbarous realm, and the prime contriver of its arbitrary policy. Black, but comely, robust, and vigorous, neck short and thick, nose large and nostrils wide, eyes inquisitive and penetrating, his was the massive brain proper to an intellect deliberate and systematic. Well found in the best idioms of his native tongue, he expressed strong, discriminative thoughts in words at once accurate and abundant. His only vanity was his English, with which he so interlarded his native speech, as often to impart the effect of levity to ideas that, in themselves, were grave, judicious and impressive.

Let me conduct the reader into one of the saloons of the palace, where we shall find this intellectual sensualist in the moral relaxation of his harem, with his latest pets and playthings about him.

Peering into a twilight, studiously contrived, of dimly-lighted and suggestive shadows, we discover in the centre of the hall a long line of girls with skins of olive,— creatures who in years and physical proportions are yet but children, but by training developed into women and accomplished actresses. There are some twenty of them, in transparent draperies with golden girdles, their arms and bosoms, wholly nude, flashing as they wave and heave, with barbaric ornaments of gold. The heads are modestly inclined, the hands are humbly folded, and the eyes droop timidly beneath long lashes. Their only garment, the lower skirt, floating in light folds about their limbs, is of very costly material bordered heavily with gold. On the ends of their fingers they wear long "nails" of gold, tapering sharply like the claws of a bird. The apartment is illuminated by means of candelabras, hung so high that the light falls in a soft hazy mist on the tender faces and pliant forms below.

Another group of maidens, comely and merry, sit behind musical instruments, of so great variety as to recall the "cornet, flute, sackbut, harp, psaltery, and dulcimer" of Scripture. The "head wife" of the premier, earnestly engaged in creaming her lips, reclines apart on a dais, attended by many waiting-women.

From the folds of a great curtain a single flute opens the entertainment with low tender strains, and from the recesses twelve damsels appear, bearing gold and silver fans with which, seated in order, they fan the central group.

Now the dancers, a burst of joyous music being the signal, form in two lines and simultaneously, with military precision, kneel, fold and raise their hands, and bow till their foreheads touch the carpet before their lord. Then suddenly springing to their feet, they describe a succession of rapid and intricate circles, tapping the carpet with their toes in time to the music. Next follows a miracle of art, such as may be found only among pupils of the highest physical training; a dance in which every motion is poetry, every attitude an expression of love, even rest but the eloquence of passion overcome by its own fervor. The music swelling into a rapturous tumult preludes the choral climax, wherein the dancers, raising their delicate feet, and curving their arms and fingers in seemingly impossible flexures, sway like withes of willow, and agitate all the muscles of the body like the fluttering of leaves in a soft breeze. Their eyes glow as with an inner light; the soft brown complexion, the rosy lips half parted, the heaving bosom, and the waving arms, as they float round and round in wild eddies of dance, impart to them the aspect of fair young fiends.

And there sits the Kralahome, like the idol of ebony before the demon had entered it! While around him these elfin worshippers, with flushed cheeks and flashing eyes, tossing arms and panting bosoms, whirl in their witching waltz. He is a man to be wondered at, stony and grim, his huge hands resting on his knees in statuesque repose, as though he supported on his well-poised head the whole weight of the Maha Mongkut itself, while at his feet these brown leaves of humanity lie quivering.

Anna Harriette Leonowens
The English Governess at the Siamese Court (1871)

Additional attractions nearby include the sanctuary of Chao Po Khun Dan, which commemorates an officer of that name who served under King Naresuan (1590–1605) and whose spirit is believed to guard the surrounding mountains; and two waterfalls, Nam Rong and Salika (best seen at the end of the rainy season).

The closest main town to Wang Takrai is Nakhon Nayok on Highway 305. At the town you take Highway 33 until its intersection with Highway 3049. Here you turn left and after 11 kilometres (6.6 miles) you reach a fork in the road; right leads to Wang Takrai two kilometres (1.2 miles) away and Nam Rong waterfall seven kilometres (4.2 miles) away, while straight on takes you to Salika waterfall.

Khao Yai National Park

Khao Yai, 205 kilometres (127 miles) from Bangkok, is the closest hill country resort to the capital. It is reached by taking Highway 1 from Bangkok to the outskirts of Saraburi where you turn east on to Highway 2 ('Friendship Highway'). About 58 kilometres (36 miles) beyond Saraburi, just before the little town of Pak Chong, a sign-posted turnoff on the right leads just over 20 kilometres (13 miles) to the park entrance (admission B25 per car).

The three to four-hour journey is best covered by hiring your own car and driver in Bangkok. Alternatively public buses leave the Northeastern Bus Terminal on Phaholyothin Road every hour for Pak Chong where minibuses ply the last part of the route to the park.

Khao Yai is Thailand's best-known wildlife and nature preserve and is an area of stunning natural beauty. The mountain vantage points offer spectacular panoramic views over densely forested valleys and hillsides. Adding to the scenic attractions are a number of waterfalls, one of which, Heo Suwat, tumbles dramatically 15 metres (50 feet) into a deep, wooded glen.

Protected within the park are bears, tigers, elephants, monkeys, wild hogs, mouse deer, sambar deer, barking deer, porcupines, civets and mongooses, along with various species of birds and butterflies. The latter are to be seen in abundance, but you'll need a good deal of luck to catch sight of the rarer animals.

Khao Yai has been laid out to afford maximum access and full appreciation of the breathtaking scenery and refreshingly cooler temperatures. A paved road cuts north-south through the park, with branch roads to Heo Suwat waterfall and to near the summit of Khao Khaeo mountain. In addition there is an extensive network of hiking trails (maps provided by the park service) and an 18-hole golf course.

Accommodation is available at the Khao Yai Motor Lodge which offers motel rooms (from B380) and bungalows (from B600) plus a camping site and dormitory rooms. The lodge is operated by the Tourism Authority of Thailand with whom reservations should be made in advance in Bangkok (tel. 282-1143/7).

Southeast

Crocodile Farm (Open daily 8 am−6 pm, admission ฿80, children half price) What is claimed as the world's largest crocodile farm−it has some 30,000 reptiles−was established in 1950 with the aim of saving the species from extinction and, at the same time, ensuring a supply of skins for the leather trade. Located 30 kilometres (19 miles) from Bangkok, it has expanded into a very tourist-oriented mini-zoo, with tigers, deer, monkeys, snakes and elephants. There are also hourly shows of crocodile wrestling (both the crocs and the keeper have been doing it for years and seem a little weary) and elephant shows. Feeding time is 5−6 pm.

Ancient City (Open daily 8.30 am−6 pm, admission ฿80, children half price) This open-air museum located three kilometres (two miles) from the Crocodile Farm occupies an 81-hectare (200-acre) site shaped to the outline of Thailand and comprises an excellent collection of full and smaller-scale replicas of the country's major monuments and temples. Each building is situated according to its actual geographic location to give an idea of regional variations in architectural style. A few structures are original and have been relocated for preservation at the Ancient City; some others are reproductions of buildings which no longer exist, such as the Grand Palace of Ayutthaya. There is also a model Thai village.

The Ancient City may sound like a typical tourist trap but, in fact, the monuments have been faithfully reproduced in full detail and do give a genuine insight into the nation's architectural heritage.

Southwest

Samut Sakhon

Also known as Mahachai, Samut Sakhon is a typical picturesque fishing port located 28 kilometres (17 miles) from Bangkok at the junction of the Tachin River and the Mahachai Canal by the Gulf of Thailand. It is interesting for its busy scene, its fish market and, by the main landing stage, a restaurant serving excellent seafood. A boat may also be hired from the fish market pier for a trip to the port's principal temple, Wat Chom Long, at the mouth of the Tachin River.

In addition to its intrinsic charm, Samut Sakhon is the destination of an unusual excursion. A narrow-gauge railway runs from Wong

Wian Yai station in Thonburi (near the Taksin Monument) to the port, and the delightful hour-long journey passes through some very pleasant wetland scenery. Departures are approximately every hour.

West

Rose Garden Resort (Open daily 8 am–6 pm, admission to gardens ฿10; to cultural show ฿140) Located on the banks of the Tachin River 32 kilometres (20 miles) from Bangkok and set amid lovely landscaped gardens, this is both a country resort (with a good standard of accommodation) and day attraction in its model Thai village and cultural show. The latter, every afternoon at three, has displays of folk dances, sword fighting, traditional ceremonies and similar examples of old-style Thai culture. In the village are work elephants and workshops for various local handicrafts. It is all a little 'instant Thailand' in character, but it is well done and good for visitors with only a short time to spend in the country.

The Rose Garden also has tennis courts, a swimming pool, an artificial lake with paddle boats and an 18-hole golf course.

Daily organized tours from Bangkok include the Rose Garden, along with Damnoen Saduak Floating Market and Nakhon Pathom (see below).

Nakhon Pathom

This town, 56 kilometres (35 miles) from Bangkok, stands on the site of one of the oldest settlements in what is now Thailand and is widely believed to have been the earliest centre of Buddhist learning in the country. Habitation of the area possibly dates back to the third century BC when the city was the capital of a Mon kingdom during the Dvaravati period (sixth to 11th century).

Sights

Dominating a vast park in the centre of the modern town is the **Phra Pathom Chedi**, the world's tallest Buddhist monument at 127 metres (417 feet). It marks the location of an ancient *chedi* constructed during the early Dvaravati period and then partially destroyed in 1057 when the city was sacked by King Aniruddha of Pagan.

It was not until the 19th century that King Mongkut decided to restore the *chedi*. However, the original structure, then standing at 40 metres (131 feet), proved to be beyond repair and Mongkut ordered a new *chedi* to be built over the ruins, the work being completed in the reign of King Chulalongkorn.

Phra Pathom Chedi is distinguished by its ringed cone atop a massive orange glazed-tile base in the shape of an inverted bowl. The proportions of the latter are so great as to belie the true height of the structure.

There are various other embellishments to the site, including a replica of the original *chedi*, while on the south side is a museum (open Wednesday to Sunday 9 am−noon and 1−4 pm) which contains some interesting Dvaravati exhibits.

A three-day temple fair is held every November in the grounds of the Phra Pathom Chedi. It is a colourful and lively affair with foodstalls, sideshows and other kinds of traditional entertainment.

The other main attraction in Nakhon Pathom is **Sanam Chand Palace**, on the west side of town. It was built as a summer residence by King Vajiravudh (Rama VI) and presents a most curious mix of English and Thai architectural styles. It is now used as government offices and is not open to the public. However, the gardens, where there is a renovated Thai *sala*, may be visited.

Kanchanaburi

Kanchanaburi, main town of the province of the same name, is best known as the location of the infamous Death Railway and Bridge over the River Kwai constructed by Allied prisoners of the Japanese during World War II (see below).

Kanchanaburi can be reached by bus or train with several daily departures from the Southern Bus Terminal (on Charan Sanitwong Road) and Hualampong Station.

Leading Bangkok travel agents operate one-day excursions from Bangkok which take in the River Kwai Bridge and other sights near town. Longer tours with accommodation at jungle resorts are also offered.

One of the best one-day excursions is the rail trip operated by the State Railways of Thailand on weekends. The special train departs Hualampong at 6.15 am on Saturdays and Sundays and stops at Nakhon Pathom, Kanchanaburi and Nam Tok with ample time for sightseeing at each location.

Kanchanaburi was built under royal patronage in the reign of King Rama III and is a prosperous little place deriving a good income from sugar cane, sapphire mining and the teak trade with Burma. It stands 129 kilometres (80 miles) from Bangkok, at the point where the Kwai Yai and Kwai Noi Rivers meet to form the Mae Klong River. Both valleys are extremely picturesque and are dotted with waterfalls and caves. The general landscape is one of lush wooded hills with an impressive backdrop of the rugged, saw-tooth mountains that form the

border with Burma. There are a number of popular scenic spots in both valleys and several 'jungle' resort hotels offering good accommodation and opportunities for river trips and jungle treks.

Sights

River Kwai Bridge After the film and the novel, the bridge over the River Kwai can appear less awesome and smaller than expected; it remains nonetheless an important historical monument. Located five kilometres (three miles) north of the town centre, the bridge is still in use (although the end of the line is only a few kilometres away), by pedestrians as well as by the little train.

During World War II the Japanese aimed to complete a rail link between Burma and Thailand (which they occupied ostensibly with the approval of the Thai government), and the bridge spanning the River Kwai was a crucial sector. Materials were brought from Java and it is estimated that as many as 16,000 POWs and 49,000 forced civilian labourers died from disease, malnutrition and harsh treatment during the rush to complete the railway.

The bridge was bombed towards the end of the war and only the curved spans seen today are original (the straight ones were later replacements for bomb damage). After hostilities ended, the railway was purchased by the Thai government, although by that time the British had begun dismantling the track at the Burmese border and the line now ends at Nam Tok station, about 60 kilometres (38 miles) from Kanchanaburi.

Kanchanaburi has two cemeteries containing the remains of Allied prisoners of war who perished during the construction of the Death Railway. The Kanchanaburi War Cemetery is on Saengchuto Road (Kanchanaburi's main street), opposite and a little way before the railway station. Here lie the graves of 6,982 POWs. The other, Chungkai War Cemetery, is to the south of town on the opposite bank of the Kwai Noi about three kilometres (two miles) from the ferry landing stage. It stands on the former site of the Chungkai POW Camp and contains the remains of some 1,750 Allied soldiers.

Located in the compound of Wat Chai Chumpol is Jeath War Museum (open daily 8.30 am−4 pm, admission ฿20). This curious little museum was built to resemble POW camp accommodation. Its exhibits of mostly photographs and paintings by prisoners tell the story of the conditions endured during the construction of the railway.

Wat Tham Mangkhon Thong The best known of Kanchanaburi's cave temples, the 'Cave Temple of the Golden Dragon' lies southwest of town on the peninsula between the Kwai Noi and Mae Klong Rivers, a couple of kilometres from the southernmost ferry point.

The main temple buildings are clustered at the foot of a hill situated a few hundred metres off to the left of the road. Next to the *viharn* is a small round pool in which an elderly nun meditates while floating on her back (weekends only, at 10 am).

From the temple compound a steep flight of steps leads up the limestone hill to a cave in front of which sits a Chinese hermit. There are two altars with Buddha images and behind the front one a narrow illuminated tunnel cuts through the mountain to exit a little further up. The passage is low and you have to crawl in places — not for the claustrophobic.

Two other cave temples that can be visited are Wat Tham Khao Laem, a half-mile or so before Wat Tham Mangkhon Thong, and Wat Tham Kao Poon, which lies about a ten-minute walk beyond Chungkai War Cemetery.

Bor-Ploy Sapphire Mines Blue sapphires found here are considered to be among the best in the world. Bor-Ploy is about 50 kilometres (30 miles) north of Kanchanaburi (can be reached by bus or car) and visitors may view the open-pit mine in operation.

Waterfalls and Caves

The valleys of both the Kwai Yai and Kwai Noi are dotted with waterfalls and caves, several of which have been groomed as local scenic spots and are popular picnic sites. The waterfalls are more picturesque than spectacular and are best seen at the end of the rainy season.

Erawan Waterfall is located in a national park in the Kwai Yai valley, about 70 kilometres (43.5 miles) from Kanchanaburi. For many Thais it is the most beautiful in the region and has seven levels with pools in between that are ideal for swimming; it can get very crowded with picnickers especially at weekends.

Khao Phang or Sai Yok Noi Waterfall is located about two kilometres (1.5 miles) from Nam Tok railway station in the Kwai Noi valley and can be reached by train from Kanchanaburi. Beautiful scenery can thus be combined with a trip on the historic Death Railway.

Kaeng Lawa Cave and Sai Yok Yai Waterfall lie further up the Kwai Noi and can be reached by boat from the Pak Saeng pier near Nam Tok. The trip, which costs ฿600–800 per boat (carries 10–12 passengers) takes 2.5 hours on the way up and 1.5 hours coming downstream. Kaeng Lawa is the biggest cave in the area, and the journey is well worthwhile for the overall beauty of the scenery.

Beaches and Island Resorts

Thailand has more than 2,500 kilometres (1,550 miles) of coastline generously provided with sandy beaches, sheltered bays and coves, and idyllic offshore islands.

The two main resort regions are the east and west shores of the Gulf of Thailand, within a few hours drive of Bangkok, and the deep south, along both shores of the Malay peninsula. It is the latter area which is less developed and more spectacular in natural scenery — long expanses of powdery white sand and soaring cliffs, jungle and rubber plantations. The culture of the South is also different and is more influenced by the proximity of Muslim Malaysia. Individual resorts are variously developed, and there is something to suit all tastes.

Pattaya

Pattaya is oft-dubbed 'Queen of Asia's Resorts'; in fact it is in a class of its own, almost defying succinct description. Let it be said straight away, it is not to everyone's liking. It is like nowhere else: brash, bawdy, colourful and alive with activity. It is arrogant and self-assured in its kaleidoscope of watersports and shore-based entertainment that almost make the beach superfluous and ensure there is never a dull moment — day or night.

In little more than two decades, what was once an untouched, gently curving bay bordered by an unpaved road with a tiny fishing village at one end has grown into Thailand's premier beach resort and an international playground. First, a string of deluxe hotels sprang up along the shore line. Then followed a largely unorganized building boom with more hotels, bars, restaurants and shops spreading well inland from the beach. At the same time sporting and recreational facilities — orthodox and unorthodox — appeared in a star-burst of activity designed to get the visitor on, above and below the water and to keep him (much is male-oriented) fully occupied on land.

Today, construction extends in all possible directions and the beach is scarcely any longer the focal point. For the simple pleasures of sun, sea and sand, people really need to venture a short distance south to Jomtien Beach, just around the headland and virtually an annex of Pattaya.

Comparatively quiet beaches and coves are located at the north end of the resort (at places such as Moonlight Beach), where one can rent bungalows and enjoy a fairly tranquil time. Moving south, however, the pace of life quickens. Here stretches the long bay with the main beach and a parallel road fronted by mostly deluxe hotels. Behind the main coast road is 2nd Pattaya Road (the back road), the two being

The Finest Silk

This village, K., was renowned for its fine hand-woven silks, and it was while I was looking for such that I came by chance across Ming and his daughter Muan. When, accompanied by Aris, I paid my first visit to Muan, on the veranda in front of the house lay fast asleep and snoring a sturdy fellow, whom, to judge from his appearance, I would have thought capable of committing a thousand crimes; it soon turned out, however, that he was far more harmless than he looked. Aris asked about the silks, but Muan only laughed, and said she had only one fine "p'ha nong," and the gentleman couldn't very well have that, as she had it on. All the others were worn out, but I could have them if I wished. However, I didn't wish, but said to Aris in some depression—for Muan was very beautiful—"Let us go," and seeing he was vexed at such a speedy departure, I simply added: "When I want silk, it is only fine silk I mean to buy."

I returned in the evening. Muan was no longer alone; her father Ming and her mother Meh Piu, both of them elderly people, sat there in grave dignity, and I felt like a man who is paying a visit, although he knows that he ought not to.

"Come up," said the father, and I climbed the ladder. Strangers are often invited to come in, although we would really like to send them off.

I felt embarrassed, for nobody spoke, and yet I had a sort of feeling that they all knew why I had come. At last Aris blurted out: "We've come about that silk. . ." "Because Muan is so beautiful," thought I to myself. Ming and his wife said nothing. Muan, too, was silent, twisting thick cigars of leaves into which she stuffed native tobacco. She wore two long, long necklaces of silver drops, which she had twisted at least twice round her brown neck, and yet they hung down far across her bosom.

When I timidly begged for my silk, papa and mamma smiled, and so did Muan's two little brothers, more broadly still, for they could not understand this business of the cloth at all. It was only after a few jokes—not really fun, but deadly earnest—had been made, that I regained my equilibrium. Mamma said that perhaps the fine silk might be sold if the gentleman did not want a worn one, but . . . she was glad that the gentleman had done her this honour, etc., but . . . as is the way of mothers, raising my hopes one minute to dash them down in cruel delight the next with one of her "buts". While Muan very kindly and nicely was showing me her spinning-wheel and some specimens of her handiwork, her mother said proudly: "My daughter is not afraid of the white master," which sounded like an invitation.

I asked the price. "Forty tikals," said the old lady, and immediately added with a laugh, "but I won't give it without the little maid inside— that makes eighty tikals."

Although I should not think much of a European mother who put a price on her daughter, it seemed to me quite intelligible that Muan should be worth these eighty tikals less forty.

My brown beauty sat on the veranda working with her bronze hands and feet, spinning and laughing whilst the pale moonlight shone between the pointed bamboo roofs out in the open and over the yellow stubble of the peaceful harvest fields. The air was soft and shimmering, still fragrant with the perfumes of the hot day only just ended, and my brain went round and round under the strain of Siamese calculations. Then Ming laughed with a meaning but undecided look, half-invitation, perhaps half-vexation, or even a threat: "Master, if you mean business here, you can have Muan."

But when I had begun to assure him that I would soon return and build a house near his, and that he could give me Muan at once, and I would send him the costly silk back again as soon as I had bought her a much finer one—as soon, I say, as I began to outdo myself in eloquent assurances, the mother all at once acted just like any other ordinary insulted mother and said, with stern brevity: "Plau—nothing of the sort!"

H O Morgenthaler
Matahari: Impressions of the Siamese-Malayan Jungle

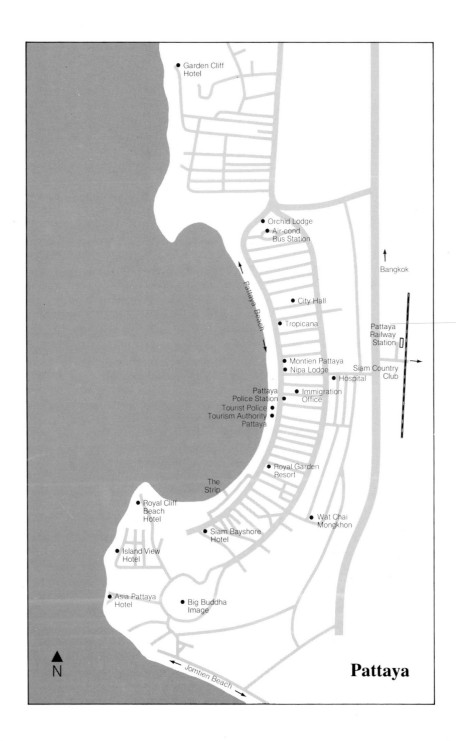

connected by numerous *sois* (lanes) and the whole area being considerably built-up. At the southern end of the bay is what used to be the fishing village and is now popularly referred to as 'The Strip'. Crammed into a small space are a jumble of open-air bars, go-go bars, discos, restaurants and shops. This is the night-time (and much of the daytime) entertainment centre, largely geared to the desires of the single male. Even if this bawdy scene is not to one's liking, 'The Strip' is worth visiting just to see it as a phenomenon and to indulge in the pleasant pastime of people-watching.

Up on the southern headland are two or three more deluxe hotels. The best is the Royal Cliff which has its own beach and watersports facilities. This could be described as the more select area of Pattaya.

While the visitor can simply laze by his hotel pool and sip on a long cool drink, there is nevertheless an irresistible pull towards a staggering range of sporting options:

Parasailing offers thrills and great views as you dangle from a parachute towed along by a speed boat. Individual operators are found on Pattaya and Jomtien beaches and charge B200—250 for a flight over the bay lasting two to three minutes.

Windsurfing is very popular at all beaches, though best at Jomtien. Hire of board and sail costs around B100 per hour, or B300 per day. Lessons may also be taken at one of several windsurfing schools.

Scuba Diving is good in the comparatively clear water and with a fair amount of coral and tropical fish to be seen. A number of dive shops in Pattaya offer tuition ranging from one-day courses to a full certificate course. These shops also rent scuba equipment.

Sailing is best at Jomtien Beach where Hobiecats and Prindles can be hired for B300—400 per hour.

Deep-sea Fishing The main centre for game fishing expeditions is Bang Saray, 18 kilometres (11 miles) south of Pattaya, where Fisherman's Inn and Fisherman's Lodge organize trips and provide the gear for going after shark, barracuda and marlin.

Waterskiing Speedboats can be hired at various beach locations for upwards of B700 per hour.

Waterscooters These machines are a pest and dangerous. Their use is officially limited to certain points on Pattaya and Jomtien beaches. They can be a rip-off as some scooters are clapped out and malfunctions may be charged to the hirer.

Tennis Many leading hotels have their own tennis courts.

Golf There is a good 18-hole, 72-par course at the Siam Country Club (facilities also at Bang Phra and the Royal Thai Navy Course). All three links are about a half-hour drive from Pattaya. Check with your hotel reception or tour counter for details of fees, transport, etc.

Shooting and Archery are available at Pattaya Sport Bazaar Building, 2nd Pattaya Road, tel. 419-642, 421-700−3. Pistols (.22, .38 and .9mm) and .22 rifles can be hired and range fee is ฿120 per person with bullets costing ฿3−9 depending on calibre. There is also an outdoor archery range where a bow and 30 arrows cost ฿100. Open 11 am−10 pm.

Bowling and Snooker Pattaya Bowl, 2nd Pattaya Road, tel. 419-466. Also at Simon Bowl, 2nd Pattaya Road.

Horseback Riding at Reo Park Range on Siam Country Club Road, five kilometres (three miles) from the Sukhumvit Highway. For beginners and experienced riders. Rates from ฿350 per hour.

After sundown there is no discernible change of pace and the choice of evening activities almost rivals that of the day — restaurants serving fresh seafood and a host of national cuisines; bars with or without go-go dancers; massage parlours, discos and, in the major hotels, rather more sedate nightclubs with live music.

A particular speciality of Pattaya's entertainment scene are transvestite shows with men impersonating famous female singers and performing song and dance routines in cabaret spectacles. The two top spots are Tiffany's on 2nd Pattaya Road and Alcazar Cabaret, which is nearby.

Getting to Pattaya

Several private bus companies operate regular daily services between Bangkok and Pattaya, the best known being Diamond Coach at 1494 New Petchaburi Road, tel. 252-4248−51, which has three departures in each direction a day at 8.30 am, 12.30 pm and 5 pm. One-way fare is ฿120. Bookings can be made at the tour counters of leading hotels from which pick-up services are offered. Alternatively the government-owned Bor Kor Sor bus company has departures every 30 minutes between 6.30 am and 8.30 pm from the Ekamai Bus Terminal on Sukhumvit Road. One-way fare is ฿50.

In Pattaya the easiest way to get around is by *song taew*, minibus pick-up trucks which ply the main roads and stop on request. Fares within the beach area should be around ฿10 and ฿20−30 for longer journeys.

Around Pattaya

Organized tours are operated to several of the places below, which offer alternatives to the usual resort fare, especially for family groups. Check with your hotel tour counter for full details.

Islands One of the easiest alternatives to the frenetic activity of

Pattaya is to make a trip out to one of the offshore islands. Most popular, and now well developed, is Koh Larn, ten kilometres (six miles) from Pattaya, to which day tours are organized at ฿250 per head. Further off and less built up is Koh Phai, to which the return boat fare is about ฿400.

Nong Nooch Village (Open daily. Cultural show 3−4.30 pm) Located 15-minutes' drive from Pattaya at KM 165 Sukhumvit Highway, this is a country resort comprising a collection of traditional Thai-style cottages set amid rolling hills and extensive landscaped gardens. Attractions include a cultural show, elephant show, mini zoo, boating on the lake, orchid nurseries and cactus garden.

Elephant Kraal (Open daily. Show 3−5 pm, admission ฿160) The place to see how elephants are captured and trained for work in the teak forests of the north, plus demonstrations of pachyderm skills and elephant rides. Popular with children. The Elephant Kraal is a short distance inland from the resort, just off the Sukhumvit Highway.

Khao Kheow Open Zoo (Open daily 7 am−6 pm, admission adults ฿20, children ฿10, plus ฿10 per car) Situated about 24 kilometres (15 miles) off the main highway from the turn off to Bang Phra Golf Course near Bang Saen, this open zoo (actually the animals are fenced in but have far more space to move around than usual) has elephants, bears, zebras, deer of various species, monkeys, wild boars and more, plus numerous kinds of birds housed in an enormous aviary. The hilly setting and woodland scenery greatly add to the pleasure of this interesting attraction.

Bang Saen Aquarium (Open daily 9 am−5 pm, admission ฿10, children half price) The coastal town of Bang Saen, just off the main highway about 45 kilometres (30 miles) north of Pattaya, is an older beach resort and still popular with Thais for day and weekend excursions. Its main point of interest for the international visitor, however, is the Aquarium and Natural History Museum at Srina-kharinwirot University, on the left on the way into town.

Chantaburi Gem Mines Day excursions can be made to the gem mining area around the town of Chantaburi, 185 kilometres (115 miles) southeast of Pattaya. Fine-quality sapphires in particular are found here, and the open-pit mines can be visited as can the gem-cutting factories in town.

Koh Samet

If Pattaya is not everyone's idea of a seaside vacation, more simple resort settings with bungalow-style accommodation can be found further down the coast around Rayong, while south of this town is the little port of Ban Phe, the hopping-off point for Koh (island) Samet.

This six-kilometre (four-mile) strip of an island with a high, vegetation-clad backbone is noted for its clear waters, coral reefs and several good beaches that dot the otherwise craggy shore. It is popular with those seeking the more typical island escape but it is by no means over-developed, and accommodation is limited mostly to comfortable though basic beach bungalows.

The most beautiful beaches are on the eastern side of the island, beginning with the splendid Haat Sai Kaeow and continuing through Tub Tim, Cho Bay, Seahorse Beach and Vongduern Beach. The only good beach on the western side is Paradise Beach, where there are bungalows and a restaurant.

Like the accommodations, watersport amenities are not well-developed, though there is windsurfing available at some beaches.

Other than its natural charm and beauty Koh Samet has a romantic connotation in its association with the 19th-century Thai poet Sunthorn Phu, who at one time retreated to the island where he produced some of his best writing.

Ferries to Koh Samet leave the pier at Ban Phe not according to any fixed schedule, but whenever a boat has sufficient passengers. The 40-minute trip costs ฿50. Vongduern Villa resort has its own ferry service. (Note: precautions against malaria should be taken prior to a journey to Koh Samet.)

Hua Hin

Located 188 kilometres (117 miles) south of Bangkok on the western coast of the Gulf of Thailand, more or less opposite Pattaya, is Hua Hin, Thailand's oldest beach resort, which offers a quieter alternative to its younger counterpart across the Gulf for family holidays.

Long known as a busy fishing port, Hua Hin first came to prominence as a resort in the 1920s when King Rama VII established a Royal Summer Palace there (it is still used by the present king). A vogue was thus established and the then first-class Railway Hotel, built in charming colonial style, was opened to cater to a burgeoning vacation traffic.

Some time after World War II, Hua Hin went into decline as a resort — the Railway Hotel languishing along with it — and it was not until the mid-1980s, when the deluxe Royal Garden Resort Hotel was built, that the beach town once again came into fashion. The Railway Hotel, now known as Hotel Sofitel Central, has been renovated in such a way as to maintain its 1920s charm while providing up-to-date facilities.

The main attraction is the beach, mostly undeveloped except for some ponies to ride and some watersports facilities offered by the

Breeding Stock

When the officials from the district came again to hold a meeting at the local temple, she waited for a long time, hoping her husband would come back with new stories to tell. And so he did. With a look of amusement, he told his wife that the Agriculture Officer called the meeting to announce that America had sent some breeding pigs and that they were to send their sows to the District Centre to be serviced. So the following dawn her husband went off taking their sow, leaving her to her thoughts the whole day, but for the life of her she couldn't imagine who America was. When her husband returned he was bragging as usual.

'It's really only a little smaller than our own water buffalo,' he related with pride.

The poor woman's trepidation grew, for if the pigs really became buffaloes then what would she do? Not sure whether he was talking about buffaloes or pigs, she asked him which he meant.

'Pigs, of course,' he affirmed.

'All right, but what do they eat, grass or bran?' she asked, still doubting.

Her husband a little perplexed replied with a chuckle, 'Well, I suppose they eat bran.'

Another day it happened again. Her husband left the house early together with their cow. The evening before, the county chief sent a man over to tell them that America had sent breeding cattle but it was a long time before she realized he meant a bull and wondered just how big it would be. She waited the whole day for her husband, anxious to hear what he would have to say. Just before dark, she knew from the sound of the wedge being driven in to hold the fence gate shut that her husband had returned.

'Giants they were, both the bull and the man,' he said excitedly. 'Enormous!'

While setting out the food, the woman listened to the story.

'As big as I don't know what. At first I thought it was a buffalo but then I looked at it and looked at it and there it was, a bull. Its hooves, its legs, horns, ears, all like a bull but what a size!' he said between mouthfuls.

'The Agriculture Officer said that the Government ordered these bulls from America because our own cows are good for nothing. They are old-fashioned, grow slowly, neither good for food nor work. And I suppose he's right.' The last sentence was offered as his own opinion and he didn't stop talking throughout supper.

'I've lived to see the day! I have seen an American. With my own eyes I saw him. The size of him! Like this.'

He turned to where his wife was sitting.

'Eh, what can I compare him with so that you can get an idea? I know, you've seen a scarecrow haven't you?'

'I have,' she agreed.

'Well, he was like that; all arms and legs with hazel eyes just like our own dog's, hair yellow-brown like dried grass.'

She went to bed early but couldn't fall asleep for thinking about the story she had heard that evening.

She thought for a long time, but finally couldn't resist putting the question.

'Grandpa,' she addressed her husband as did her grandchildren.

'What is it?' her husband answered quietly.

'Why did they send that scarecrow over?'

'Uh,' her husband sighed deeply.

'They sent him for breeding just like the bull, didn't they?' she asked further.

There was silence for a moment. 'That's right. That must be it.'

'And are they sending him to our District?'

'Not yet I think. Now they're just using him in Bangkok for the women there,' he replied, tickled by the idea.

'Oh!'

'What do you mean by "Oh"?' her husband queried.

'Oh, erh, that is I feel sorry for, well I feel sorry for those Thai cows, that's all grandpa,' she faltered.

'Well for Thai people too.'

The last sentence hardly disturbed the stillness of the dark night.

Khamsing Srinawk, The Politician and Other Stories

Fruits of Thailand

Thailand produces an abundance of fruit. Besides common varieties, such as banana, papaya and pineapple, there are a number of succulent fruits to be found in any market during the appropriate season:

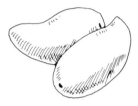

Mango (*Mamuang*) — Peeled, they can be eaten when still green or when ripe. Taken with sticky rice, the latter type is a popular Thai dessert — *khao neo mamuang*. Season: March–May.

Rambutan (*Ngok*) — An oval-shaped red-and-green-coloured fruit with bristles on the skin. Inside is a juicy, whitish meat, reminiscent of the lychee, around a seed. Season: July–September.

Durian (*Turian*) — Most distinguished by its pungent — and to some obnoxious — smell, this fruit has a hard green/yellow-brown shell with sharp thorns. Inside, the light yellow meat is very rich and sweet. An acquired taste. Season: April–June.

Jackfruit (*Ka-noon*) — A large, thick-skinned fruit with soft thorns. Break in half and eat the yellow, rather tangy meat but not the large seed. Available throughout the year.

Mangosteen (*Mongkhut*) — This fruit has a thick, dark purple skin encasing a delicate, juicy flesh with a pleasantly tart flavour. The pulp is in segments and the fruit is eaten by first breaking it in half. Season: April–September.

Longan (*Lamyai*) — A small round fruit with a thin but tough skin, closely related to the lychee. The transparent white meat, around a black seed, is delicious. Season: July–October.

Pomelo (*Som-oh*) — Rather like an over-sized grapefruit, though sweeter and drier. Peel off the light green pithy skin and eat in segments. Available throughout the year.

Custard Apple (*Noina*) — Light green and shaped rather like a hand grenade, this fruit has a white, sweet meat formed in segments and with lots of black seeds which should not be eaten. Eat by breaking in half. Season: July–September.

Rose Apple (*Chomphu*) — A delicate-looking pinkish-white fruit of which the skin and crisp meat can be eaten but not the small seed. Best when chilled. Season: April–July.

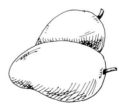

Sapodilla (*Lamut*) — A plum-shaped fruit with a brown skin. Peel and eat the very sweet meat but not the seed. Available throughout the year.

Royal Garden Resort. Otherwise Hua Hin's sporting attraction is golf, on a good 18-hole course.

The town goes about its business with scarcely a regard for the tourist. It is interesting for its fishing port, its bustling night bazaar and a handful of simple but good restaurants serving local seafood. The place is small enough to walk around although trishaws are a plentiful and inexpensive means of transport. Most tourist activity is concentrated around the two main hotels, just south of the town centre, but there are no sights as such, except for the quaint railway station with its royal waiting room which must be one of the most attractive little stations anywhere.

Getting to Hua Hin

Diamond Coach (Bangkok tel. 252-4248−51) operates a daily air-conditioned bus service, departing Bangkok at 9 am and taking about three-and-a-half hours to reach Hua Hin. (The same bus stops at Cha-am.) In the opposite direction, the bus leaves Hua Hin at 2.30 pm. Round-trip fare is ฿350. Alternatively, government-run buses leave the Southern Bus Terminal in Thonburi every hour.

Sights

Hua Hin's hinterland, with picturesque hills, jungle, lakes, sugar cane and pineapple plantations, offers touring possibilities.

For the culturally oriented, the historic town of **Petchburi**, 65 kilometres (40 miles) north, is worth a few hours. A centre of artistic output during the Ayutthaya period, it boasts a handful of beautiful old temples (note the superb mural paintings in Wat Yai Suwannaram and Wat Ko Keo Suttharam), a hilltop palace built by King Mongkut, and Khao Luang Cave which enshrines a number of Buddha images.

South of Hua Hin, 23 kilometres (14 miles) away, is the port of **Pran Buri** and close by the national park of **Khao Sam Roi Yot** ('Mountain of 300 Peaks'). The latter is a magnificent place, comprising forested hills, waterfalls, caves, beaches and coves, and a profusion of flora and fauna. Of particular note among the caves is Phraya Nakhon, where a shrine has been erected to commemorate a visit by King Rama V.

For details of day excursions around Hua Hin, the visitor is best advised to contact the tour counter at the Royal Garden Resort.

In addition, the town of **Cha-am**, 26 kilometres (16 miles) north of Hua Hin, offers another resort choice with good beaches and first-class accommodation at the Regent Cha-am or the Beach Garden Resort.

Phuket

Situated off the west coast of the southern peninsula and connected to the mainland by Sarasin Bridge, Phuket Island, 900 kilometres (560 miles) south of Bangkok, is currently Thailand's finest resort. At 21 kilometres (13 miles) wide and 48 kilometres (30 miles) long it is roughly the same size as Singapore, and is the epitome of a tropical island paradise — the warm waters of the Andaman Sea, a choice of uncluttered beaches of silver-white sand and a backdrop of hills clothed in a profusion of tropical greenery.

At the same time, Phuket has been gradually groomed for tourism over a number of years and although not developed to the detriment of the environment, it does offer deluxe creature comforts to complement the joys of nature. The island province first became wealthy because of its tin mining industry, but tourism is probably a more important source of income today.

Phuket town is not impressive. Its old architectural mix, still visible, is a generally pleasing blend of European-colonial and Chinese styles and reflects a lengthy history of cultural mingling. Otherwise it offers two first-class hotels — The Merlin and The Pearl — a little shopping, a few restaurants and a bit of nightlife. As far as sights go, Put Jaw, Phuket's oldest and largest Chinese temple (dedicated to Kuan Yin, the Goddess of Mercy), on Ranong Road is worth a visit. The classic evening pastime is a stroll up Phuket Hill for a fine view of the town and surroundings (for Phuket hotels, see pages 206–8).

There is a considerable variety in beach locations, both in terms of scenery and in facilities available. All the best spots are on the west coast:

Mai Khao is the longest beach and the place where, during November to February, giant sea turtles come ashore to lay their eggs.

Nai Yang is part of Nai Yang National Park and prettily fringed by casuarina trees. It offers a blend of beach and parkland.

Surin is an attractive spot, although the beach slopes sharply and undercurrents can make swimming hazardous, especially during the April to September monsoon season. This is a good spot for watching Phuket's famed sunsets. Just inland is a nine-hole golf course.

Laem Sing Beach and Kamela Bay are tranquil and scenic, ideal for a quiet, simple time.

Patong is the island's most developed beach, with facilities for windsurfing, boating, snorkelling and fishing. Long-tailed boats may also be hired here for trips along the coast. The beach slopes gently and is a good place for children to swim.

Karon and Kata Beaches both boast fine sand and clear water; good for snorkelling.

Nai Harn is Phuket's southernmost beach, with a majestic sweep of sand, a lagoon behind and an attractive bay. Laem Prom Thep headland on the southern tip is an excellent vantage point for sunset watchers.

Rawai is definitely not one of Phuket's best beaches, but is interesting for the fishing village inhabited by the so-called Sea Gypsies — *Chao Talay* — a people who depend on the sea for their livelihood and who, with a language of their own, are believed to be related to the Andaman Islanders.

The East Coast is the more sheltered but more rugged side of the island where a handful of pearl farms are to be found. In the northeast Thalang District is the lovely Tone Sai Waterfall and national park where the jungle tree growth is beautiful and totally unspoiled. A little to the north of the park is Wat Phra Thong where there is a half-buried Buddha image — legend has it that all attempts to unearth it fully have met with misfortune.

Phang Nga Bay

The most interesting and popular day excursion from Phuket is to Phang Nga Bay, off the mainland 93 kilometres (70 miles) from Phuket. Travelling by long-tail boat, one first passes through mangrove river swamps before entering the bay rising out of which are numerous limestone rock formations. Some rise sheer from the water, others are humped or jagged, and all are strange and hauntingly beautiful. The boat also enters caves and grottoes and makes a lunch stop at a Muslim fishing village built entirely on stilts over the water. A visit can also be made to the most famous of the rocky outcrops, Khao Ping Gan, now commonly dubbed 'James Bond Island' as it was the location for the movie *The Man With the Golden Gun.*

Organized tours to Phang Nga may be booked at any of the main resort hotels in Phuket. To do it yourself, travel across Sarasin Bridge and on to Khok Kloi where the way to the Custom House Pier is signposted.

About 30 kilometres (17 miles) from Khok Kloi is the cave temple of Tham Suwan Ku Ha, a vast cavern enshrining Buddha images. A stop at the cave is included on the organized tours from Phuket to Phang Nga Bay.

Phi Phi Islands

These two islands lying east of Phuket have a natural beauty even more stunning and pristine than that of the resort and offer beaches, caves and rocky cliffs. Organized tours are available, or you can hire your own boat from Rawai Beach and other locations.

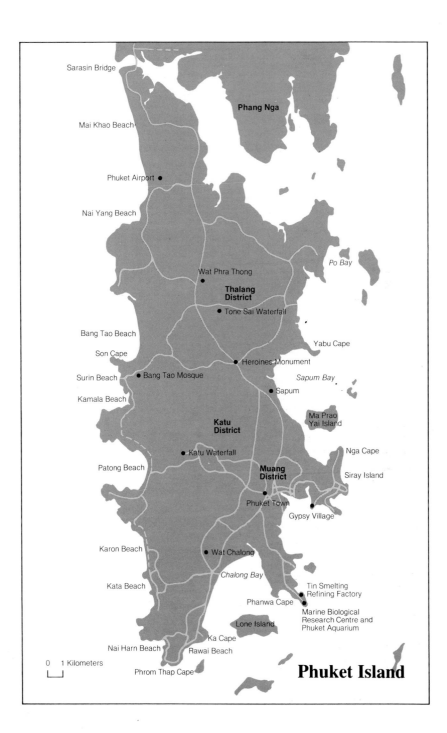

Sarasin Bridge

Mai Khao Beach

Phuket Airport ●

Nai Yang Beach

Phang Nga

Po Bay

Wat Phra Thong
●
**Thalang
District**

● Tone Sai Waterfall

Bang Tao Beach

Son Cape

Surin Beach

● Bang Tao Mosque

Kamala Beach

Yabu Cape

Heroines Monument

Sapum Bay

● Sapum

Ma Prao
Yai Island

**Katu
District**

● Katu Waterfall

Patong Beach

**Muang
District**

Nga Cape

Siray Island

●
Phuket Town

Gypsy Village

Karon Beach

● Wat Chalong

Chalong Bay

Kata Beach

Tin Smelting
Refining Factory

Phanwa Cape

Marine Biological
Research Centre and
Phuket Aquarium

Lone Island

Ka Cape

Nai Harn Beach   Rawai Beach

0   1 Kilometers

Phrom Thap Cape

Phuket Island

Phuket Aquarium

Operated by the Phuket Marine Biological Research Centre, this is a well-maintained aquarium with a good collection of tropical fish, mammals and crustaceans. Ideal for children and for putting a name to all those species of marine life you see while scuba diving or snorkelling.

Phuket Aquarium can be reached by taking the bus from the market in Phuket town marked either 'Aquarium' or 'Markham Bay'.

Getting to Phuket

Thai Airways operates several flights (by B-737 jet) daily between Bangkok and Phuket. Flying time is just over an hour. There are air-conditioned buses from the Southern Bus Terminal in Thonburi. The land journey takes 14 hours.

Koh Samui

This large island off the east coast of the southern peninsula, 560 kilometres (348 miles) from Bangkok, has long been popular with budget travellers. Accommodation facilities (mostly beach bungalows) are increasing and more infrastructure is being developed, but for the moment Koh Samui remains an unspoiled island hideaway, offering something of the Robinson Crusoe experience. The islanders themselves, mostly fishermen and coconut farmers who pursue a lifestyle which has been largely unchanged for centuries, are friendly people and help make the island a place apart.

Characterized by beaches of powdery white sand, crystal clear waters and a hinterland of fresh green coconut plantations and rice paddies, Koh Samui is one of a group of 80 islands of which only four are inhabited. Thus while lazing peacefully on a beach is the main attraction, fishing boats can be hired for excursions to outlying islands.

There are several beaches to choose from — Lamai and Chaweng on the east coast being the most popular — and a serviceable road rings the island. Apart from windsurfing at Chaweng Beach, sporting facilities are limited.

Nevertheless Koh Samui is not without other attractions, and excursions (either by hiring your own motorbike or by taking a *song taew* minibus) into the hilly green interior offer a pleasant change of scene. Principal among the sights are two picturesque waterfalls, Hin Lad which is about three kilometres (two miles) from the island's port and main settlement of Ban Ang Thon, and Na Muang, some ten kilometres (six miles) from the town.

There is also the temple of Wat Hin Ngu on neighbouring Fan Island, which is connected to Koh Samui by a causeway. Here there is a large statue of the seated Buddha set high on a rocky point.

Getting to Koh Samui

Bangkok Airways operates seven daily round-trip flights directly between the capital and Koh Samui. Alternatively, if the direct flight to Samui is fully booked, Thai Airways operates four daily flights to Surat Thani, where you can catch the ferry across to Koh Samui. The State Railways of Thailand operates one express and two rapid trains daily with early evening departures from Bangkok, arriving in Surat Thani early the following morning. Fares range from ฿125 in third class to ฿630 for a first-class sleeper. Alternatively, there are four daily bus departures from the Southern Bus Terminal which take about 11 hours to cover the journey. The one-way fare is ฿225. From Surat Thani it is a short bus ride to the port of Ban Don, from where there is a regular ferry service to Koh Samui; the journey takes just over two hours.

Songkhla

Songkhla is not the classic resort. It does have a stretch of sand, the long casuarina-fringed Samila Beach, but it is more of a spot for taking in the local scene than actually swimming. Much of Songkhla's fascination stems from its location on a peninsula, 1,274 kilometres (792 miles) south of Bangkok, with the Gulf of Thailand on the east and Songkhla Lake (Thale Sap), actually an inland sea and the largest body of water in Thailand, on the west. Large vessels cannot enter Songkhla port, though the waterfront still bustles with fishing and coastal craft. This is home to the colourfully and highly-imaginatively painted fishing boats for which the region is famous.

Songkhla's long and often turbulent history stretches back more than a thousand years. The town has at various times been an outpost of the Srivijaya empire, a pirate stronghold and a Chinese settlement; it was an important trading post in the early days of European interests in the Far East.

Sights

Today Songkhla is a somnolent kind of place, overshadowed by the brash city of Hat Yai 28 kilometres (17 miles) away. Few monuments of the past remain; there are, however, some good examples of Sino-Portuguese shophouse architecture along Nakorn Noak Road and

Nakorn Nai Street. The racial mix of its inhabitants — Thai, Chinese and Malay Muslims — also helps preserve a distinct and colourful atmosphere.

Wat Matchimawat This 400-year-old temple off Saiburi Road houses a small museum of art objects collected from around the region.

Songkhla Museum, located on Rongmuang Road, is housed in a splendid old building of Thai-Chinese architecture that was formerly the official residence of regional commissioners. It has some notable exhibits, particularly from the Srivijaya period.

Khao Noi is a small hill not far from the Samila Hotel and commands fine views of the town. There is also a topiary garden at the top.

Khao Tang Kuan is another hill to the west of Khao Noi where there are ruins of an old chedi and again, excellent panoramas of Songkhla.

Samila Cape At this pine-fringed scenic spot located three kilometres (two miles) from the town market on Ratchadamnoen Road are food stalls and beach chairs for relaxing and admiring the view.

Songkhla Lake There are opportunities here for fishing, picnics and boat excursions to the islands. Among the latter, Koh Yor is worth visiting for its local cotton weaving cottage industry and two old temples, Wat Khao Bo and Wat Thai Yor. Koh Maew and Koh Nu — Cat and Mouse islands — are also easily accessible. The most convenient place to hire boats is from the pier near the market on Chana Road.

Wat Koh Tham This curious hilltop temple, located about two kilometres (1.5 miles) beyong the Samrong intersection on Highway 4, is noted for its highly revered Buddha footprint and statue of the Reclining Buddha.

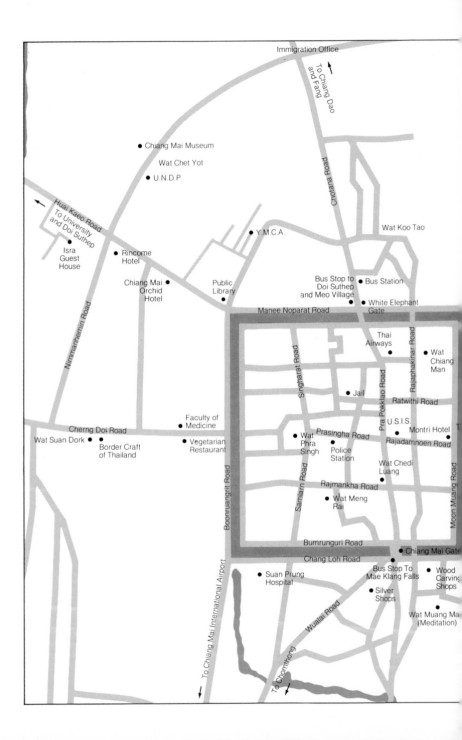

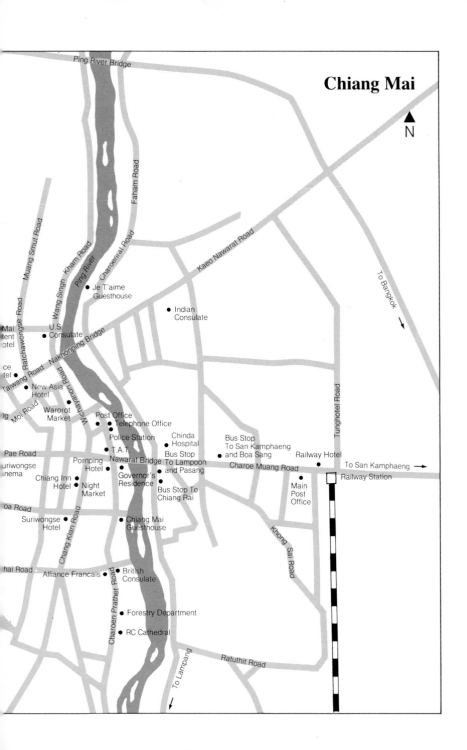

Chiang Mai

N

Ping River Bridge

Faham Road

Kaeo Nawarat Road

To Bangkok

Charoenrai Road

Kham Road

Ping River

Muang Smut Road

Wang Singh Road

Je T'aime
Guesthouse

Indian
Consulate

Nakhonping Bridge

Ratchawongse Road

Mai
dent
otel

U.S.
Consulate

ce
tel

Taiwang Road

Wichayanon Road

Tunghotel Road

New Asia
Hotel

ng Moi Road

Warorot
Market

Post Office

Telephone Office

Police Station

Chinda
Hospital

Bus Stop
To San Kamphaeng
and Boa Sang

Railway Hotel

Pae Road

T.A.T.

Bus Stop
To Lampoon
and Pasang

Charoe Muang Road

To San Kamphaeng

uriwongse
nema

Pornping
Hotel

Nawarat Bridge

Railway Station

Chiang Inn
Hotel

Night
Market

Governor's
Residence

Bus Stop To
Chiang Rai

Main
Post
Office

oa Road

Chiang Klan Road

Chiang Mai
Guesthouse

Suriwongse
Hotel

Khong Sai Road

hai Road

Alliance Francais

British
Consulate

Charoen Prathet Road

Forestry Department

RC Cathedral

To Lampang

Ratuthit Road

Chiang Mai and the North

The North is different from other regions of the country: different in topography, in culture and in ethnic make-up. In contrast to the bordering central plains the area is mountainous, with ranges that are distant offshoots of the Himalayas. All peaks — the highest is Doi Inthanon at 2,595 metres (8,514 feet) — are, however, well below the tree-line and are stunningly clothed in a profusion of vegetation. This is teak country and although the wood has now been over-exploited, forests are still part of the natural scenery. Cutting paths north to south between the mountains are the four principal rivers of the North — the Ping, Wang, Yom and Nan — which flow through enchantingly beautiful valleys. Adding to the scenic beauty are numerous caves and waterfalls.

Northern Thailand is also ethnically distinct, with a strong Burmese influence — most readily witnessed in the art and architecture of the region — while Lao strains are also discernible. Then paralleling mainstream society are the hilltribe minorities, people of different ethnic origins who retain their own languages, religions, customs, styles of dress and semi-autonomous way of life. Their cultural identity remains largely intact and although the encroachment of towns does affect their daily life to an extent, they inhabit separate villages where the pattern of existence has scarcely changed.

The numbers of hilltribe people inhabiting the North has been variously estimated at between 250,000 and 500,000. There are seven major tribes:

Karen Of Tibetan-Burman stock, the Karen are indigenous to southeastern Burma and are the most populous of the various tribes. Their villages are found throughout most of the region, except in the eastern section. The costume of the women (hilltribe men now mostly sport the dress of the ordinary Thai farmer) is a long, loose one-piece dress. Colours are worn only by married women; single girls dress in white.

Meo Also called Hmong, the Meo have a high profile and seem less shy than other tribespeople. They are a minority group from southern China (where they are called Miao) and have settled mostly in Chiang Mai, Chiang Rai, Phrae, Lampang and Mae Son provinces. The women wear jackets and pleated skirts over trousers decorated with coloured embroidery. They also make and wear large chunky silver jewellery.

Once numerous in the highlands of Vietnam and Laos, the Meo have been subjected to harassment and persecution in recent years by the Vietnamese in retaliation for their anti-communist activities

(allegedly CIA-supported) during the Indochina War. Many who have managed to flee into Thailand have been resettled in the United States, and several states now boast active and significant Meo/Hmong communities.

Akha One of the smallest, poorest and most underdeveloped of the tribes, the Akha originally migrated from Yunnan in southern China by way of the Shan states of Burma and have settled mostly in Mae Chan and Mae Sai districts north of Chiang Rai.

Lahu Originally of Tibetan stock, though migrating to Thailand via China, the Lahu comprise four principal groupings in the country, all of which are referred to by the Thai name of 'Muser'. They are scattered in small numbers throughout the region, and tend to be more nomadic than the other tribes. Traditional dress for the women is a long, narrow skirt and jacket. Broad strips of coloured cloth adorn collar, breast, sleeves and hem.

Lawa Possibly of Mon-Khmer stock, the Lawa inhabited the region long before the Thais. Today they are concentrated to the south and west of Chiang Mai. Dress is usually a rather plain smock-like garment, dark blue for married women, white for young girls. Pipe smoking among the women is common.

Lisu From their homeland in southern China, numbers of Lisu migrated to northern Thailand some 60 years ago. They, like the Meo, tend to cultivate the opium poppy and are found mostly in the mountain areas around Chiang Dao, Fang, Mae Hong Son and Tak. They are among the most colourful of the tribespeople, the men sporting long-sleeved black jackets with silver decoration, and either bright green or blue baggy pantaloons. The women dress in colourful long-sleeved blouses reaching to the knees and worn over trousers. Their typical headdress is a broad turban with long tassels.

Yao Migrating to Thailand via Burma and Laos in the first half of this century, the Yao originally hail from central China. They have maintained many Chinese traditions and are generally regarded as being culturally superior to the other tribes. They are most commonly found in the northern part of Chiang Mai Province, Chiang Rai and Mae Hong Son. Yao women look resplendent in colourfully embroidered black blouses and trousers, with lengths of coloured cloth hanging from the waist. They also wear large black or dark blue turbans and, most distinctively, a red or pink 'puff' around the neck of the blouse.

The hilltribe population adds variety and colour to the ethnic mix of the North, but their presence is not without problems for the central government. Mostly migratory, modern political boundaries mean little to them. Except for the Karen and Lawa, the tribespeople have traditionally cultivated the opium poppy as their cash crop. Also a problem is their slash-and-burn farming which has led to the destruction of forests and watersheds with consequent soil erosion. At the same time their standard of living is extremely low.

In an effort to eradicate such problems and to raise living standards, a number of government projects have been instigated to provide medical, social and educational aid and, most significant, to try to introduce alternative cash crops, replacing opium with fruits and vegetables which can grow well in the North and for which there is a good market.

Trekking

Hilltribe villages are found throughout the North and the visitor is generally made welcome. Inevitably those settlements closest to towns present a less authentic picture of tribal life. Consequently, the best way to see the hilltribes is by trekking to the more isolated villages. There are numerous trekking agencies in Chiang Mai offering trips from one night to one week and longer.

An average-length trek lasts four days/three nights and costs about ฿500−600 per person. A typical trip begins with a bus or truck ride to the starting point. Days are spent walking at a reasonably easy pace for no more than three to five hours. Nights are spent in the houses of hilltribe villages, and food is provided and prepared by the trek guide.

The most popular trekking area is around Chiang Rai, although Mae Hong Son is now also a favourite district. The former, while more frequented, does perhaps offer the greater variety of tribes.

A note of warning: visitors are best advised to arrange treks through a registered agency which will have qualified guides who know the area and the people. Trekking on your own is not advisable as, while security is pretty good, the jungle is not the city and hold-ups have been known to occur.

Chiang Mai

Chiang Mai, nearly 700 kilometres (450 miles) north of Bangkok, is Thailand's second city, although it is less than one-fortieth the size of the nation's capital.

Popularly known as 'The Rose of the North', the city is attractively sited on the banks of the Ping River and lies in a fertile plain partially surrounded by forested hills. Founded in the 13th century, Chiang Mai is one of the country's oldest settlements and manages to retain much of its separate cultural heritage along with a leisurely old-world charm.

It is a treasure house of the art and architecture of the Lanna period, an important centre for traditional handicrafts and an ideal base from which to explore the northern region.

Modern development has not bypassed Chiang Mai and the city has expanded considerably in the last few decades, spreading well beyond the confines of the old fortified gates and moat which are still to be seen. Motorized traffic now tends to clog the narrow inner city streets and, with an increasing importance as a commercial and administrative centre, Chiang Mai has undoubtedly lost some of its former charm. Nevertheless, new building has not obliterated the sight of ancient temples, craftsmen still ply their time-honoured trades, and there is little of the frenetic air that typifies Bangkok.

Moreover, the cultural attractions of the North are not artificially preserved simply for the tourist industry. With a long, largely independent history and, until the 20th century, comparative isolation, the people of the region retain a very real sense of their own identity and a pride in their heritage. Such individuality indelibly colours the character of Chiang Mai.

What latter-day changes there have been are mostly for the best.

Opium pod being harvested for its deadly but valuable sap

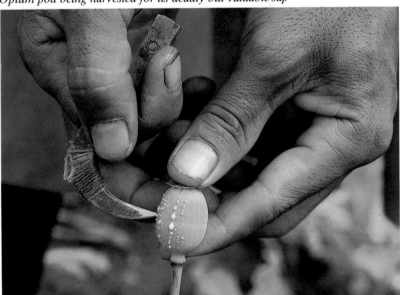

The city now offers an excellent range of accommodation, including half a dozen first-class hotels; restaurants and places of evening entertainment are, if not as numerous as in Bangkok, sufficient to give ample choice; and transport around the region, by road and, in the case of major towns, by air, is comprehensive and convenient.

All this means that while there is plenty to see and do in Chiang Mai itself, the city is also the perfect place for making excursions into the surrounding countryside, to neighbouring towns, and to hilltribe villages.

Getting to Chiang Mai

Chiang Mai is easily accessible from Bangkok by air, rail and road.

Thai Airways Company operates several daily jet flights between the capital and Chiang Mai. Flying time is just under one hour.

The State Railways of Thailand operates two trains a day from Bangkok's Hualampong Station. A rapid train departs at 3 pm, arriving in Chiang Mai the following morning at 5.15 am, while the better express service departs at 6 pm and arrives at 7.50 am. The latter has a restaurant car and first-class air-conditioned sleepers. Reservations should be made at least a week in advance. Call the State Railways in Bangkok at 223-0341.

For travel by road, public air-conditioned and ordinary buses depart from Bangkok's Northern Bus Terminal on Phaholyothin Road for Chiang Mai and other towns in the North. Private coach services from Bangkok to Chiang Mai are operated by Chiang Mai Golden Tours, tel. 245-4647. Journeys are overnight, leaving Bangkok in the evening and arriving in Chiang Mai in the early morning (for Chiang Mai hotels, see pages 200−1).

Sights

As with Bangkok, temples come at the top of Chiang Mai's sightseeing list. However, with the city's greater age and distinct history, there is more architectural variety as traditional northern styles are blended with Burmese influences.

Wat Chiang Man Located on Rajaphakinar Road, this is probably Chiang Mai's oldest temple, reputedly built by King Mengrai who resided there while his capital was being constructed. It comprises a *bot*, two *viharns* and a *chedi* in Lanna style although the elephant buttresses around the base show Sri Lankan influence. Enshrined in one of the *viharns* are two especially revered Buddha images. One is the small crystal figure known as Phra Setang Khamani, which is believed to have been presented to Queen Chama Devi of Haripunchai (modern Lamphun) in the seventh century and taken to Chiang Mai after the defeat of that city by King Mengrai in the 13th century. The other image is the bas-relief figure of Phra Sila which is possibly of Indian origin and more than a thousand years old.

Wat Phra Singh Located on the corner of Singharat and Rajadamnoen Roads, this temple was constructed in 1345 by King Pha Yu who built the large *chedi* to enshrine the ashes of his father, King Kam Fu. The main point of interest here is the old chapel behind and to the left of the main temple buildings, which enshrines the important Buddha image of Phra Singh Buddha. It is in early Chiang Saen style and was brought from Chiang Rai in 1400. The chapel itself is a good example of traditional northern architecture, while its interior walls are decorated with some fine narrative mural paintings. Also of interest in the compound is the ornate 14th-century scripture repository to the right of the modern *viharn*.

Wat Chedi Luang With its main entrance on Phra Pokklao Road, Wat Chedi Luang is renowned for its enormous, though partially ruined, *chedi* which was first raised in 1401, extended to a height of 86 metres (283 feet) by King Tilokaraja in 1454, and then damaged by an earthquake in 1545 and never restored. The *viharn* is also interesting as one of the best examples of northern monastic architecture.

Wat Chet Yot Situated outside the city centre on the Superhighway close to Chiang Mai Museum, this temple was built by King Tilokaraja in 1455 and derives its name from its seven (*chet*) spires. The design is a copy of a temple at Pagan, Burma, which itself is a replica of the Mahabodhi Temple in Bodh Gaya, India, where the Buddha achieved enlightenment. Wat Chet Yot is historically important as it was where the eighth World Buddhist Council was convened in 1477.

Wat Suan Dork 'The Flower Garden Temple', as its name translates, stands in a large compound off Suthep Road which was originally the pleasure gardens of the early Lanna kings. The *chedi* contains some important relics and the *bot* houses a good Chiang Saen-style Buddha statue cast in 1504, but the temple buildings have been extensively restored and lack architectural interest.

Wat Umong Located outside the city centre off Cherng Doi Road, this largely ruined temple complex occupies a tranquil setting (behind is a small open zoo) which makes it an attractive sight. Of the original structure, built by King Mengrai in 1296, there remains ruins of the *chedi* and, beneath it, underground catacombs where monks once meditated.

Wat Koo Tao Sited off Chotana Road, Wat Koo Tao is fascinating for its curious *chedi* shaped like five melons (or perhaps alms bowls),

Labour Negotiations

Next morning, feeling very king-like, I repaired to the office to see a veritable crowd of courtiers in the shape of headmen, fierce-elephant mahouts and coolies awaiting audience of me. Seating myself at Orwell's desk, I commanded our Siamese clerk to let them in one by one.

"Lord," said the first, a headman, "I desire a rise in my pay."

It struck me as rather curious that he should want one the first day Orwell was absent, and I took up the notes that Orwell had left for my guidance. One or two employees were marked for rises, but certainly not this gentleman.

"That," I answered, "thou canst not have."

"Then do I desire to leave the service of the Great Company," said the headman, respectfully but firmly.

I hesitated for a second. I had yet to feel my way, to learn the ropes, and were I to begin by losing one whom I knew was the firm's best headman, it would be a bad start. Was the man bluffing, or wasn't he?

I took my decision. To give in would be arrant weakness. And what about that kingship of mine? I said. "Thou canst go to-morrow."

He salaamed and withdrew. The next was the head compound coolie.

"Lord," said he, "I wish for an increase in my wages."

"Impossible," I answered.

"Then I wish to go."

"Certainly," I replied without hesitation.

He departed. After him appeared a fierce-elephant mahout.

"Lord," said he, "it is time my wages grew."

"It is not yet time."

"In that case it is my wish to return to the home of my parents over the hills."

"May thy journey be safe and thy parents pleased to see thee," was my answer.

And so it went on the whole morning. By the time the tiffin hour had arrived, every single employee of any consequence had signified his decision to leave on the morrow as I would not grant him a rise. Since there was nothing else to be done, I walked over to Orwell's bungalow and sat down to lunch.

Though I had taken over Orwell's cook, an excellent Lao we had nicknamed the Prince, and the meal was therefore as good as one could get out in the wilds, I didn't enjoy it in the least, for inwardly I was confoundedly worried. You couldn't train a head coolie, must less an elephant headman, in a week or even a month, and with the whole of the work of the forest coming to a standstill I should be very properly in for the sack. On the other hand, to give in would prove equally fatal; the men would feel, I reflected, that they could do anything they liked with me, and directly Swan or the F.M. saw the rise in the pay-sheet, which would be enormous, again I would get into trouble.

After tiffin, instead of returning to the office, I remained in the bungalow, pretending to read a book but in reality just sweating, both mentally and physically. The men, I guessed would be holding a palaver in the coolie lines, and I was wondering what the outcome would be.

After tea I strolled leisurely back. As I entered the office from the bungalow side, I saw with satisfaction that the whole pack of them were crouching in the porch at the other side, evidently in mind for an interview. I kept them waiting purposely for another half-hour, busying myself on some rice and chili accounts, then told the Siamese clerk that I would see the first.

The headman appeared and salaamed deeply:

"Lord," said he, "I think that my pay is sufficient as it is. Wherefore do I not desire to leave the services of the Great Company."

"Very well," I answered, looking as though the matter was of very little interest to me one way or the other.

"Lord," said the head compound coolie, "my wages are all that I could wish for."

"Lord," said the fierce-elephant mahout, "my wages have grown enough. Wherefore shall the home of my parents across the hills not yet see me."

And so on down through the whole pack of those brown children. By nightfall I had the satisfaction of having proved myself King.

Reginald Campbell, Teak-Wallah *(1935)*

one on top of the other in descending order of size. It is believed to have been built in 1613 to contain the ashes of a Burmese ruler of Chiang Mai.

Chiang Mai National Museum Located on the Superhighway close to Wat Chet Yot, the museum is open daily (except Monday and Tuesday) 9 am—noon and 1—4.30 pm. It houses a small but good collection of Buddha images from various periods plus, on the upper floor, displays of hilltribe costumes and traditional northern household utensils.

Tribal Research Centre On the campus of Chiang Mai University, the Tribal Research Centre contains a fascinating collection of hilltribe artifacts. Open Monday to Friday 8.30 am—4.30 pm.

Chiang Mai Zoological Park Located on Huai Kaeo Road near the university, this is Thailand's largest zoo. It occupies extensive, attractively landscaped grounds and holds over 500 animals. Open daily from 8 am to 5 pm.

Handicrafts and Shopping

Chiang Mai is Thailand's largest centre for cottage industries and numerous types of handicrafts make shopping a big attraction. Best buys include woodcarving, silverware, lacquerware, celadon pottery, hand-painted paper umbrellas and *objets d'art*, notably those from Burma. (Note: faking antiques is a well-developed business in Chiang Mai. The reproductions are good provided they are presented and priced as such and not as the genuine article.)

Workshops where you can see all these items being made and make purchases are scattered around town, while the road to Bor Sang (the 'umbrella village') and San Kamphaeng (noted for silk and cotton weaving) is a 13-kilometre (eight-mile) stretch lined with various handicraft centres.

The **Night Bazaar** on Chang Klan Road in the city centre is a popular place for browsing for hilltribe handicrafts and low-priced souvenirs. Business gets going after 6 pm. Chiang Mai's traditional markets are Warorot Market (fresh produce and general goods) at the intersection of Chiang Mai and Wichayanon Roads, Suan Buak Hat (flowers) by Suan Prung Gate, and Somphet Market (fresh fruit) which borders the moat in the northeast corner of the city.

Eating Out

Chiang Mai offers the whole gamut of dining possibilities, from Thai cuisine to other Oriental and European specialities. And eating places vary from the simple (but good) food stalls to gourmet restaurants.

The north's famous culinary speciality is a *khantoke* dinner. This consists of a number of dishes, somewhat more spicy than usual due to Burmese influence, taken with sticky rice as well as plain rice. In traditional style one dines sitting on the floor around a low table (*khan* means bowl and *toke* is a small round table). Performances of typical northern dances usually accompany the meals. *Khantoke* dinners are a speciality at the Diamond Hotel, 33/10 Charoen Prathet Road.

Excursions from Chiang Mai

Several travel agents operate half- and full-day excursions from Chiang Mai, tours which can generally be booked through hotel travel counters. Alternatively most places are served by public buses or pick-up truck minibuses which are inexpensive to hire (approximately ฿500 per day, depending on negotiations with the driver).

Doi Suthep

The forested peak of Doi Suthep has several attractions. Located near the top, and reached by a flight of 290 steps, is the beautiful temple of Wat Phrathat. A short distance from the foot of the mountain is Phuping Palace, the summer residence of the Royal Family. Only the palace's well-maintained gardens are open to the public. The Meo village of Ban Doi Pui is also found on Doi Suthep, but it is the most frequented hilltribe settlement in the entire north and a veritable tourist trap. Still, if you have no time to visit villages further afield, it does give some idea of hilltribe lifestyles.

Doi Inthanon and Mae Klang Waterfall

Situated 58 kilometres (36 miles) from Chiang Mai, Thailand's highest mountain, Doi Inthanon, stands in a national park. A road leads up to the summit from where there are fine panoramic views, while the entire area is noted for beautiful scenery, splendid flora and fauna and a number of hilltribe villages.

At the foot of Doi Inthanon is Mae Klang Waterfall, a popular local beauty spot where the falls tumble picturesquely over three rocky ledges.

Mae Sa Valley

Located 14 kilometres (nine miles) north of Chiang Mai near the village of Mae Rim, this is an area of great scenic charm (sometimes

called 'little Switzerland'). The natural beauty has been augmented by attractive landscaping and the provision of resort facilities.

Lamphun

Lying 26 kilometres (16 miles) south of Chiang Mai, this pleasant little town was the site of Haripunchai, capital of an independent Mon kingdom founded in 660 by Queen Chama Devi and defeated by King Mengrai in 1281. The town's most important monument, Wat Phra That Haripunchai, is a fascinating temple complex originally founded in 1044. Its many buildings and *chedis*, both ancient and modern, are exquisite examples of Dvaravati and Chiang Saen styles. It is an intriguing place to wander around.

Lamphun's other major sight is Wat Ku Kut (commonly known as Wat Chama Devi) on the western side of town. The temple dates from the eighth century, although the present main buildings are modern. The attraction, however, is the eighth-century *chedi* of Suwan Chang Kot, an excellent example of the late Dvaravati stepped pyramid style, and the tenth-century (rebuilt in the 12th) octagonal Ratana Chedi. Both structures were restored in the 1960s.

Lampang

Situated at the junction of Highways 1 and 11, about 100 kilometres (60 miles) southeast of Chiang Mai, the provincial capital of Lampang is an interesting town occupying both banks of the Wang River. It has boomed considerably in the last few years, though it still has some horse-drawn carriages (the only place in Thailand that has) and manages to cling to vestiges of its more leisurely past.

Sights

Wat Phra Kaeo Don Tao Located on the right bank of the Wang River, this temple complex is a fine blend of Burmese and Thai styles. Next to the sturdy *chedi* is an extremely ornate 18th-century Burmese-style shrine, while beside this is an equally superb old-style Thai hall. Also of note is a small museum to the left of the gateway. Wat Phra Kaeo Don Tao is famous as being the temple where it is believed the Emerald Buddha was enshrined for 32 years on its protracted journey from Chiang Rai to Chiang Mai.

Wat Sri Chum Closer to the town centre on the left bank of the Wang, this is another good example of Burmese architecture. Both the *bot* and *viharn* show fine decorative work especially in their carved eaves and pediments.

Wat Sri Rong Muang This temple again displays the Burmese style and has a visually dazzling exterior with eaves and woodwork painted yellow, red and blue.

Wat Pha Fang Otherwise undistinguished, this *wat* is noted for its tall *chedi* which is unusually surrounded by seven small chapels, one for each day of the week.

Wat Phra That Lampang Luang This large walled temple complex lies some 15 kilometres (ten miles) south of Lampang off Highway 1 near the village of Ko Kha. It comprises a number of buildings and numerous treasures, including an 'emerald' Buddha image said to have been carved from the same block of green jasper as the famous statue in Bangkok's Wat Phra Keo. A temple is supposed to have occupied the site since 496 but the present buildings date from the 18th century. Wat Phra That Lampang is somewhat off the beaten track, though its relative isolation only enhances its attraction.

Young Elephant Training Centre Some distance north of Lampang is this centre where elephants are trained for work in the government-owned teak forests. Their numbers are dwindling — as are the teak stands — but a few pachyderms are still employed as the most efficient and cost-effective means of hauling timber from the forest to roadside collection points. The centre is open to visitors who, in the morning, can see elephants from three to five years old and upwards being taught work skills by their *mahouts* and displaying their various talents. Demonstrations are held daily (except during the March–May hot season) from 6 to 9 am. Organized tours are available from Chiang Mai travel agents (see page 195).

Longer Excursions

Mae Hong Son

This tranquil little town lies in a picturesque valley surrounded by high forested hills 369 kilometres (229 miles) northwest of Chiang Mai close to the Burmese border. It is just half an hour from Chiang Mai by air, although the long horseshoe sweep of the road offers a more exciting journey through some spectacular scenery as the way winds up, down and around the mountains (a nine- to 12-hour journey, however).

Sights in this sleepy little place include the temple-topped Doi Kong Mu, a 424-metre (1,360-foot) hill on the edge of town from where there are panoramic views of Mae Hong Son and the mountains all around; Wat Phra Non and Wat Kham Kho, two Burmese-style temples near the foot of Doi Kong Mu; Wat Hua Wiang near the market; and Wat Chong Kam and Wat Chong Klang, two more Burmese-style temples attractively sited on the edge of the town's small lake. The morning market (busiest between 6 and 8 am) is also fascinating to stroll around.

Chiang Rai

Chiang Rai can be easily reached from Chiang Mai, 168 kilometres
(105 miles) to the south, by either bus or plane. But a more thrilling
approach is by river from Tha Thon. This little settlement, due north
of Chiang Mai beyond Fang, is located on the banks of the Kok River
down which long-tail boats daily ply the four- to five-hour journey to
Chiang Rai. Boats leave around noon and so you need to make an
early morning start from Chiang Mai by bus. The river trip takes you
through some delightful scenery and can be more leisurely covered in
three days/two nights by custom-built bamboo rafts, though you need
to order your raft about a week in advance (all-in costs are around
฿2,500). Warning: passengers on the Kok River have occasionally
been held up and robbed. The chances of this happening are slight,
though you are advised to carry only minimal cash and valuables.

Sights

Chiang Rai is a pleasant, quiet provincial capital, first founded in 1262
by King Mengrai. Few vestiges of its long history remain, however,
and the town's main interest lies in a handful of temples. Of these,
Wat Phra Keo on Trirat Road is the most famous as it is said that the
famous Emerald Buddha was discovered here when lightning cracked
the *chedi* and exposed the hidden statue. Also of note is **Wat Ngam
Muang**, atop a small hill, where an ancient brick *chedi* enshrines the
remains of King Mengrai, placed there by his son in 1318.

Otherwise Chiang Rai is primarily a good base for exploring the
surrounding countryside. Several of the town's small guesthouses
organize local treks to hilltribe villages.

Chiang Saen, site of an ancient power centre from which King
Mengrai began his consolidation of the north and his Lanna kingdom,
is of considerable historical importance as well as being an attractive
spot on the banks of the Mekong River. It lies 60 kilometres (37 miles)
northeast of Chiang Rai and can be reached by public bus. The town
has a scattering of ancient ruins of which the most notable are **Wat Pa
Sak**, which has an excellently restored *chedi* and is located off to the
left as the road turns right to enter town; **Wat Phra That Chom Kitti**, a
hilltop temple with a possibly tenth-century *chedi* and good views over
Chiang Saen; and **Wat Chedi Luang**, located in town next to the
museum and noted for its 58-metre (186-foot) high octagonal *chedi*.

Just upstream from Chiang Saen, the Ruak River flows into the
Mekong forming the so-called 'Golden Triangle', the point where the
borders of Thailand, Burma and Laos meet. It is a scenic spot
somewhat spoiled by the large modern sign loudly announcing 'The
Golden Triangle'.

The Chiang Saen Guesthouse is the best place to stay and here you can hire bicycles and motorcycles for exploring the pretty countryside and scattering of hilltribe villages.

Nan

Nan, 332 kilometres (206 miles) east of Chiang Mai, is a 45-minute flight from the capital of the north, and a tiring seven-hour ride by bus. Located on the west bank of the Nan River, the town is a thriving but unspectacular provincial centre and is mostly interesting for its old temples.

Sights

Nan is known for its annual boat race held on the river at the end of Buddhist Lent (October/November). It is an exciting and colourful event with local teams of oarsmen paddling long, sleek naga-prowed racing boats and vying for the honours. There is also a lively fair held at this time.

For the other attractions of the town it is best to begin sightseeing at the National Museum which, despite the few exhibits, does give the background of Nan's history which dates back to the 14th century.

Wat Chang Kham Vora Viharn Located opposite the museum, this *wat* is noted for its *chedi*, constructed in 1406 though restored several times since. The two *viharns* are unexceptional but the monks' residence houses a 15th-century gold statue of the walking Buddha.

Wat Phumin On the other side of the road a short walk beyond Wat Chang Kham Vora Viharn is Nan's best-known temple, Wat Phumin, built in 1596. The *viharn* of Wat Phumin is constructed on a cruciform pattern with steps leading up to superbly carved doors on each of the four sides. Inside is a giant centrepiece of four Buddha images facing each of the cardinal points, while the walls are decorated with mural paintings which are fascinating for their scenes depicting northern provincial life.

Wat Phaya Phu The buildings are of little interest but two excellent bronze statues of the walking Buddha are enshrined here. These were cast at the same time as the gold image in Wat Chang Kham and two others now housed in the museum. The life-size figures flank a giant seated Buddha, though the latter in no way detracts from their beauty.

Wat Suan Tan This temple has a 40-metre (130-foot) high *prang*, while its much-restored *viharn* enshrines the 500-year-old Buddha image of Phra Chao Thong Tip. This bronze statue was cast on the orders of King Tilokaraja of Chiang Mai in 1449 after he had conquered the town. It is said that he gave the people just seven days to find sufficient metal and set a 100-day time limit for refugee Sukhothai craftsmen to cast it.

Wat Phra That Chae Haeng Located a short distance southwest of town on the opposite bank of the Nan River, this is a walled temple dating from the 11th century and is impressive for its 55-metre (176-foot) high *chedi* and its *viharn* with architecture revealing Laotian influence.

Tak

Situated a little more than half-way between Bangkok and Chiang Mai, and with a first-class hotel (Viang Tak), the little town of Tak is a good overnight stop for travellers going north by car. It is also a convenient base for excursions.

Pleasantly situated on the banks of the Ping River, Tak's main claim to fame is as the place where King Taksin of Thonburi was once a governor, hence the first part of his name (his original surname being simply Sin). This illustrious hero is remembered in a statue and pavilion in his honour at the northern end of town on Phaholyothin Road.

On the opposite side of the road is Tak's other main sight, **Wat Bot Mani Sibunruang**, notable for its gold-crowned *chedi* and old *viharn* in typical northern style.

From Tak, excursions may be made to **Mae Sot**, an interesting little border town which faces Burma across the Moei River; to **Kamphaeng Phet**, where there are numerous ruins of the old city that was once a satellite of Sukhothai; and to the ruined city of Sukhothai itself.

Sukhothai

Sukhothai, site of the first Thai capital, was founded in the first half of the 13th century. It lies roughly between the end of the central plains and the start of the northern region, about 350 kilometres (215 miles) southeast of Chiang Mai. The modern town, a ten-minute drive east of the ruined city, is neither generous in its accommodation facilities nor well-located on major communication lines. As mentioned above, the ancient site is conveniently reached by road from Tak. Alternatively, the best gateway is the town of **Phitsanulok**, 55 kilometres (35 miles) southwest, which has a domestic airport (flights from Bangkok and Chiang Mai) and is on the main northern railway line.

Phitsanulok also has two or three good-quality hotels and one major sightseeing attraction, **Wat Phra Sri Ratana Mahathat**. This is a fascinating temple complex and is most famous for the highly-revered Buddha image of Phra Buddha Chinaraj, a superb example of late

Sukhothai sculpture magnificently housed in the main chapel. Also of note are the doors of the chapel which are decorated with mother-of-pearl inlay, and generally Wat Mahathat (in common abbreviation) is worth viewing in some detail.

Sights

Whether you make your base in Tak, Phitsanulok or one of the little hotels of modern Sukhothai, you should allow at least a full day for exploring the ruins at **Sukhothai Historical Park**, Thailand's single most important historical site. Covering 70 square kilometres (27 square miles), the park is a well-maintained area of lawns, paths and

Elephants

For most people the elephant is an endearing creature, a popular draw at the zoo or circus. For the Thais it enjoys a much more exalted status as an animal that has made significant contributions to national life.

Throughout Thai history the elephant has served man in various capacities, both practical and figurative. In olden times, war elephants were effective fighting machines, the forerunner of the tank and the mount of royalty who would enter into single combat on the back of a specially trained beast.

The white or albino elephant has for centuries been the sole property of the king, the possession of one or more presaging well for the success of the reign.

In representational form the pachyderm has been depicted in countless murals and illustrated manuscripts; it was once engraved on Thai coins, and from 1819 to 1917 a white elephant on a red background was the national flag. The animal is further featured in Buddhist legend. One of the *Jataka* tales relates how the Buddha in a previous life was born as a white elephant with six tusks emitting magical rays.

On the popular level there are hundreds of sayings and superstitions about the pachyderm. One common belief holds that it is lucky to walk under the creature's belly, a practice supposed to be specially efficacious in ensuring a pregnant woman an easy childbirth.

But it is as a work animal that the elephant has contributed most. It is still employed in the dwindling teak forests of the North where it remains more efficient than machines in hauling and stacking timber.

Several elephant training schools are operated in northern Thailand and here, in the early mornings, the visitor can get a close-up view of pachyderms being put through their paces by their *mahouts*, or handlers. These establishments serve a practical purpose though: as the number of work elephants is declining, they are also showgrounds for visitors.

Elephants begin schooling between the ages of three and five, and require five to six years of dedicated tuition before they are fully versed in the various skills needed for forestry work. They are employed more as a partner of man than as slave, and generally an elephant will remain with one *mahout* until it is retired, like man, at around the age of 60.

Despite their enormous size, pachyderms are delicate creatures and require great care. Because of the heat, they work mornings only, while during the worst of the hot season they are given a vacation.

The days of the working elephant are now numbered, though for the time being it remains a characteristic sight in the North, a reminder of a long and illustrious contribution to the cultural fabric of Thailand.

ponds set against a background of wooded hills. Within the confines of the old ramparts and moat are more than 20 major monuments, while others are scattered in every direction beyond. Most of the remains (recently restored under a ten-year UNESCO-backed programme) are of temples of which the *chedis* are the best-preserved free-standing monuments.

The best starting point is **Ramkamhaeng National Museum** (open Wednesday to Sunday). It lies off to the left (coming from modern Sukhothai) of Highway 12, which cuts east-west through the ancient site. Here there is a good collection of sculpture (note especially the statue of the walking Buddha which was the finest achievement of Sukhothai artists) and other artifacts which give a useful introduction to the period.

From the museum it is just a few steps to the heart of the ancient city. The following is a list of only the not-to-be-missed monuments and does not exhaust sightseeing possibilities:

Wat Mahathat Lying to the west of the museum, this is the biggest and most magnificent of Sukhothai's temples and is dominated by a *chedi* in the form of a lotus bud, a style unique to the period. On the surrounding platform are four *stupas* and four *prangs*, while the base is decorated with stucco figures of Buddhist disciples. To the sides are two giant statues of the standing Buddha, and on the eastern side are twin rows of pillars, the remains of the *viharn*, and a platform with a large image of the seated Buddha.

Wat Sri Sawai The three distinctive and well-restored *prangs* of this temple, southwest of Wat Mahathat, are in Khmer style and it is possible that the building was begun as a shrine to the Hindu god Shiva before being converted to Buddhist use. Initial construction thus likely dates from the late 12th or early 13th century, before the founding of the Thai City.

Wat Trapang Ngoen Situated west of Wat Mahathat, this ruin comprises the remains of a *viharn* and a *chedi* picturesquely sited on a small island in the middle of an ornamental pond.

Wat Sra Sri Another island temple northwest of Wat Mahathat, this temple is notable for its Sri Lankan-style *chedi* and the remains of a large *viharn* containing a stucco Buddha statue.

Wat Phra Phai Luang Located outside the city walls about a ten-minute walk beyond the northern gate, the extensive remains here rival those of Wat Mahathat in importance. Its Khmer-style *prang* (there were originally three, but only one remains standing) likely predates the Thai period. In all, three separate stages of construction can be discerned as the once Hindu shrine was converted to a Buddhist temple. In front of the *prang* are the ruins of a *viharn* and a *chedi*, the base of the latter being decorated with stucco Buddha images. Nearby is a *mondop* enclosing ruined statues of the walking, standing, sitting and reclining Buddha.

Wat Si Chum This is a huge square *mondop*, southwest of Wat Phra Phai Luang, enclosing an enormous stucco-over-brick Buddha statue in the attitude of 'subduing mara'. Called Phra Achana in King Ramkamhaeng's stone inscription, the image measures 11.3 metres (36 feet) wide at the lap. Inside the surrounding *mondop* is a narrow passage where the ceiling is decorated with beautifully engraved slabs illustrating scenes from the *Jataka* tales. The passage is closed to the public but some of the engravings can be glimpsed through the iron-grill gate.

Wat Saphan Hin Situated on the top of a small hill two kilometres (1.25 miles) west of the city, this temple has an impressive 12.5-metre (40-foot) high statue of the standing Buddha. Only some columns and part of a brick wall behind the image remain of the original enclosing *viharn*.

Wat Chetupon This is the most important monument lying to the south of the ruined city. Its main feature is a *mondop*, now in ruins, enshrining Buddha images in the four postures — standing, sitting, walking and reclining.

Wat Chang Lom This temple is the major sanctuary on the eastern side of the historical park. It has an excellent bell-shaped *chedi* in the Sri Lankan style with elephant buttresses (now disfigured) surrounding the square base.

Wat Chedi Sung and Wat Trapang Thong Lang These two monuments lie just south of Wat Chang Lom. The former is distinguished by a splendid *chedi* of which the upper part is bell-shaped and the base is in the form of a stepped platform. The latter temple, located nearby, has a square *mondop* as its main sanctuary which is remarkable for the stucco decoration on the outer walls.

Si Satchanalai

Situated about 70 kilometres (45 miles) north of modern Sukhothai on the west bank of the Yom River, Si Satchanalai was a sister city of Sukhothai. It was governed by a son of the Sukhothai monarch and served as a secondary power base.

Si Satchanalai was a much smaller city than Sukhothai and its buildings were less grand, but the place is more compact and thus it is easier to get an impression of what the original city must have been like.

Sights

Si Satchanalai's most commanding monument, standing a little aside
from the main cluster of ruins, is **Wat Chang Lom**. Described in King
Ramkamhaeng's stone inscription as the 'temple surrounded by
elephants' (*chang*) and probably dating from the late 13th century, its
principal feature is a large bell-shaped *chedi* raised on a square base
which is decorated with elephant buttresses, now rather disfigured.

A short distance to the south, opposite Wat Chang Lom, are the
extensive ruins of **Wat Chedi Chet Thaew** — seven rows of *chedis*
likely constructed to contain the ashes of the city's rulers. Of special
note is the stucco image of the Buddha under a *naga* on the side of the
central structure facing Wat Chang Lom. Traces of the original stucco
decoration are also visible on some of the other *chedis*.

Located closely in a southeast line are the remains of **Wat Uthayan
Yai** and **Wat Nang Phaya**, while to the east of Wat Chedi Chet Thaew
a *chedi* is all that survives of the chapel and adjacent palace.

Atop each of the two hills on the northern side of the site are the
ruins of **Wat Khao Phanom Phloeng** and **Wat Khao Suwan Khiri**. The
former is the easier to reach, via a steep flight of steps, and comprises
laterite columns, a seated Buddha and a *chedi* behind the sanctuary.
The latter is distinguished by a large, finely proportioned *chedi*. Both
vantage points command panoramic views of the ancient site and
surrounding countryside.

Although not strictly part of Si Satchanalai proper, some two
kilometres (1.25 miles) away from the main site, on the banks of the
Yom River, are the impressive ruins of **Wat Phra Si Ratana Mahathat**.
It dates from the height of Si Satchanalai's development in the late
13th century, although it was extensively restored and altered during
the Ayutthaya period.

Set out in an east-west line, the temple complex comprises two
seated Buddha statues, a large Sri Lankan-style *chedi*, a central *prang*
along with a brick and stucco seated Buddha, a standing Buddha
partially embedded in the ground and the columns of the main *viharn*.

Of greatest interest is the *prang*, a magnificent structure showing
Khmer architectural influences that were again popular during
Ayutthaya times and which testify to later restoration work on top of
the original base. Adjoining the *prang* are the remains of the sanctuary
where on one side is a splendid laterite and stucco high-relief of the
walking Buddha. It is tucked away and overshadowed by the soaring
tower, but it should not be missed as it is a masterpiece of its kind.

Natural Light

By the time the tide had risen the night had fallen thick and dark, and the dense shade of the jungle, through which the canal led us, made it yet thicker and more dark. Great fern leaves, ten or fifteen feet in height, grew dense on either side, and fanlike, almost met over our heads. Above them stretched the forest trees. Among them rose the noise of night-birds, lizards, trumpeter-beetles, and creatures countless and various, making a hoarse din, which, if it was not musical, at least was lively.

But the jungle, with its darkness and its din, had such a beauty as I never have seen equalled, when its myriad fire-flies sparkled thick on every side. I had seen fire-flies before, and had heard of them, but I had never seen or heard, nor have I since then ever seen or heard, of anything like these. The peculiarity of them was—not that they were so many, though they were innumerable—not that they were so large, though they were very large—but that they clustered, as by a preconcerted plan, on certain kinds of trees, avoiding carefully all other kinds, and then, as if by signal from some director of the spectacle, they all sent forth their light at once, at simultaneous and exact intervals, so that the whole tree seemed to flash and palpitate with living light. Imagine it. At one instant was blackness of darkness and the croaking jungle. Then suddenly on every side flashed out these fiery trees, the form of each, from topmost twig to outmost bough, set thick with flaming jewels. It was easy to imagine at the top of each some big white-waistcoated fire-fly, with the baton of director, ordering the movements of the rest.

George B Bacon
Siam: The Land of the White Elephant (1892)

The Northeast

The Northeast — Issan as the Thais call it — is in many ways the most traditional part of the country. It is also the poorest, with its agriculture-based economy adversely affected by low-yield soil and the vagaries of nature, there being either too much or too little rain. In spite of, or perhaps because of, a relatively low living standard, cultural traditions — in music, folk dances, festivals, legends and local dialects — are better preserved here than elsewhere in Thailand.

The region thus has a distinct character of its own, and this is further coloured by a strong Laotian influence. The Thais are ethnically more closely related to the Lao than to any of their other neighbours, and this serves to strengthen the individuality of the Northeast. The culture and character of Issan is most readily witnessed in the many colourful festivals celebrated annually, quite a few of which are unique to the Northeast.

Issan is bounded in the north and east by the Mekong River, which defines the border with Laos. To the south the Dongrak mountains separate Thailand from Kampuchea. Most of the region comprises a vast plateau where subsistence farming is carried out. Because of its size the area can appear empty but, while village life is typical, there are a number of large towns dotted about and the Northeast has some of the most populous settlements in the country. (Both Khorat and Khon Kaen are large, fast-growing urban centres.)

The region has for long served as a pool of unskilled labour for Bangkok and a stream of young people, especially girls, has swelled the capital's population. The migration continues, but local economic conditions are improving. Various irrigation and agriculture development projects are being implemented. Issan began to be opened up in the late 1950s when the so-called Friendship Highway (Highway 2), a joint Thai-US project, provided an all-weather road from Saraburi all the way up to Nong Khai on the Laotian border. A significant, albeit temporary, economic boost came during the Vietnam War when towns such as Udon and Ubon hosted huge American air bases.

Archaeologically and historically, Issan is of prime importance. Just a few years ago, prehistoric finds at Ban Chiang yielded evidence of an advanced bronze-using culture that has set archaeologists rethinking the pattern of world civilization. In the realm of recorded history, the Northeast possesses the finest surviving examples of ancient Khmer monuments to be seen outside of Kampuchea — for the time being, that effectively means to be seen anywhere at all.

Issan also has its scenic attractions. Khao Yai National Park lies between Khorat and Bangkok, while in the northeast proper Loei Province is well known for its natural beauty, in particular around Phu Kradung mountain. And over to the east, in an area once the stronghold of communist insurgents, there is some fine hill country at Phu Pan near the town of Sakhon Nakhon. Then, of course, there is the Mekong, one of the world's longest and certainly one of the most famous and evocative rivers.

Getting to Issan

One of the reasons why comparatively few visitors make a trip to the Northeast is because of the sheer size of the region and the fairly long distances between major places of interest. Access from Bangkok, however, is good. Within the region a network of excellent roads, usually free of heavy traffic, connects all the main cities and towns, and local bus services are comprehensive.

Thai Airways operates flights from Bangkok to Khon Kaen, Udon and Ubon, and from Khon Kaen there are feeder services to Sakhon Nakhon and Loei. The privately-owned domestic airline, Bangkok Airways, has regular flights from Bangkok to Khorat.

The State Railways has two daily express trains leaving Bangkok for the Northeast: one goes via Khorat to Ubon, while the other branches north at Khorat to terminate at Nong Khai. Both departures are in the early evening.

For travel by bus there are numerous daily services from Bangkok's Northern Bus Terminal on Phaholyothin Road to all principal towns in Issan.

Khorat

More correctly named Nakhon Ratchasima and popularly dubbed 'Gateway to the Northeast', Khorat, 256 kilometres (160 miles) northeast of Bangkok, is the region's largest town and commercial centre. It is not a particularly prepossessing city, though with a handful of good hotels, it is a convenient base from which to make excursions to various Khmer historical sites.

Sights

The best-known and best-preserved Khmer ruins in the Northeast are at Phimai, located ten kilometres (six miles) east of Highway 2 from the turnoff 49 kilometres (30 miles) northeast of Khorat. On the way, a stop should be made to take in the smaller monument of **Prasat Phanom Wan** which lies five kilometres (three miles) down a side road (signposted in English) off to the right of Highway 2, 15 kilometres (nine miles) out of Khorat.

This attractive ruin of a 1,000-year-old Khmer sanctuary stands in an isolated walled compound where only the rustle of the wind in the trees disturbs the peace. The main buildings are in pretty good condition and comprise a vaulted antechamber leading to a rectangular-based tower. Characteristic Khmer architectural devices are evident in the false and true windows, and over the north entrance to the sanctuary tower a fine carved lintel remains intact.

Untypically, the temple is still in use and the interior is adorned with several Buddha images including a large statue of the standing Buddha inside the main tower.

Phimai (open daily 7.30 am−5 pm, admission Ƀ20) is the showcase of Thailand's Khmer monuments, being an extensive temple complex restored by the Fine Arts Department of the National Museum to the fullest extent possible.

During its heyday in the late 12th century, the original settlement of Phimai occupied an artificial island on the Mun River, and a number of remains are scattered about the present town. The old southern gateway (Pratu Chai), for instance, is an obvious landmark at the end of the main street. The principal sanctuary tower and accompanying buildings, however, stand within a massive walled compound in the centre of town.

Although the origins of Phimai are a matter of debate among historians, the extent of the ruins clearly indicates a role of some importance. The sanctuary tower, with adjoining antechamber (*mandapa*) and superb porticoes on three sides, is a magnificent structure and a splendid testament to the master builders of the Khmer empire. Fine proportions are complemented by carved lintels and other decorative work, while the pyramidal roof is imposingly supported by *garudas* and features guardian figures interspersed with *nagas*.

On the left of the inner courtyard, as you enter by the southern gateway, are the *prang* of the Hindaeng Sanctuary and, behind, a Hindu shrine (the temple complex formerly served both Hindu and Buddhist functions). To the right is the *prang* of the Bhromathat Sanctuary. These structures likely date from the reign of Khmer monarch Jayavarman VII (1181−1201) and a stone figure of this king, now in the National Museum, Bangkok, was found at Prang Bhromathat.

In the outer courtyard are four corner ponds representing the sacred rivers of India, which served ceremonial purposes.

For a detailed look at Khmer stonework, the open-air museum

(open daily 8.30 am – 4.30 pm, admission free), on the left as you cross the bridge over the Mun River on the approach to town, has a good collection of carved lintels gathered from Phimai and other Khmer sites in the Northeast.

Just before the bridge a track leads off to the left to Sai Ngam park where a large banyan tree makes an impressive spread of foliage.

Prasat Phanom Rung and Prasat Muang Tam are two ancient Khmer sites east of Khorat, quite close to the Kampuchean border. To reach them take Highway 224 heading southeast out of town, and after 28 kilometres (17 miles) turn left on to Highway 24. At 118 kilometres (73 miles) from Khorat (about 15 kilometres (nine miles) beyond the Buriram turnoff) a signposted turnoff on the right leads 12 kilometres (7.5 miles) to Prasat Phanom Rung.

Currently undergoing extensive restoration, Prasat Phanom Rung is in some ways more impressive than Phimai. The temple complex is not as large but is comparatively well preserved, and enjoys the advantage of a spectacular hilltop location from where there are panoramic views of the plateau below and, to the south, of the mountains bordering Kampuchea.

The impressive wide paved approach to the sanctuary leads to a cruciform terrace with *naga* balustrades from which rises a grand staircase, split into three landings and of impressive proportions.

Dating mostly from the 12th century, the principal buildings within the walled compound consist of a *gopura*, a main gateway structure with lateral room, and a square-based sanctuary tower with entrances and antechambers at the four cardinal points. On its eastern side the tower is linked to a magnificent *mandapa*, a rectangular chamber which precedes the main entrance to the sanctuary. This structure is one of the finest of its kind to have survived. Also noteworthy are the pediments and carved lintels of interior and exterior doorways, and the decorative friezes on walls and pillars.

The ruined temple of **Prasat Muang Tam** lies at the bottom of the hill about five kilometres (three miles) from Prasat Phanom Rung in a direct line. The road, however, is anything but a direct line and access is complicated. One can either take the road that follows straight on from the T-junction after coming down the hill from Phanom Rung, or retrace the route back to Highway 24, continue east to the little town of Prakhon Chai and turn right on to Highway 2075. Either way, one is likely to get lost and it is necessary to ask someone the way to Ban Chorakae Mak, the village nearest the ruins.

Prasat Muang Tam was built in the tenth century. The temple is surrounded by laterite walls with gateways at the four cardinal points, and the outer courtyard features L-shaped ponds in each corner. The main sanctuary in the inner courtyard originally comprised five *prangs* but the central one collapsed some time ago. A couple of carved lintels can still be seen and, while badly dilapidated, the remains are sufficient to give a good impression of the original appearance.

Touring the Northeast

The Khmer ruins to be seen within striking distance of Khorat are the most important sights of Issan, for both historical significance and visual impact. There is, however, a good deal more to see in the region as a whole, and the more adventurous traveller can conveniently cover the area by following the roughly circular route outlined below. It is best done by car, though public bus services connect all the towns.

Khon Kaen

Some 190 kilometres (118 miles) north of Khorat on Friendship Highway, this large, modern town is important as the development centre of the Northeast. It is spacious and has a generally pleasing air of prosperity, reflected for the traveller in the two or three first-class hotels.

The only place of real interest is the museum (open Wednesday to Sunday 9 am–noon and 1–4 pm, admission ฿10) which has a good collection of Ban Chiang pottery.

Otherwise Khon Kaen's main tourist attraction is its annual Silk Fair held in the first week of December. The town is in the heart of one of the most important producing areas for *mutmee* silk, perhaps the best-known Northeast handicraft. The fair combines an exhibition of the silk industry with opportunities to buy the material and, of course, all the entertainment traditional to an upcountry celebration.

If you are not in the area in time for the Silk Fair, the whole process of the silk industry, from cocoon through spinning and dyeing to weaving on hand looms, can be seen at the village of Chonnabot, about 50 kilometres (30 miles) south of Khon Kaen.

Udon Thani

This town, 120 kilometres (74.5 miles) north of Khon Kaen, was once the site of the world's largest air base when US servicemen were stationed here during the Indochina War. That presence brought a temporary and slightly dubious prosperity in the form of a burgeoning entertainment industry, mostly girlie bars and massage parlours. All that has long since disappeared and Udon has reverted to its quiet former self and has little to interest the traveller. It is, however, a convenient base for exploring this part of the plateau.

Fifty-six kilometres (35 miles) to the north, the Friendship Highway terminates at **Nong Khai** on the banks of the Mekong across from the Laotian capital of Vientiane. This was once the main crossing point for entry into Laos, but the border is currently closed.

At **Si Chiang Mai**, 45 kilometres (28 miles) west of Nong Khai, there is a good view across the Mekong to the rooftops of Vientiane.

To the west of Udon lies **Loei** Province, notable for its beautiful natural scenery, especially at **Phu Kradung National Park**, a little over 100 kilometres (65 miles) south of the provincial capital. The name translates as 'bell mountain' and the park occupies a tabletop plateau at an elevation of between 1,200 and 1,500 metres (3,850 and 4,800 feet). The area is covered mostly by evergreen forest which supports a wealth of wildlife, including several rare species of birds. Hiking trails provide convenient access.

East of Udon about 50 kilometres (30 miles) along Highway 22 and a bit off to the left is the tiny village of **Ban Chiang**, now world-famous for the archaeological discoveries made there in the early 1970s. The finds, including skeletons, tools, distinctively decorated pottery and metal artifacts, have been dated as up to 6,000 years old. This predates sites in China and Mesopotamia as the earliest known evidence of an agrarian, bronze-making culture, and suggests that the Khorat plateau may be one of the possible 'cradles of civilization'.

The excavation work has all been completed, but in the compound of Wat Poh Si Nai, on the far edge of the village, two pits have been left open to display numerous finds *in situ*, which gives one a feel for the thrill of archaeological discovery. There is also a small museum in the village (open Wednesday to Sunday, 9 am−noon and 1−4 pm).

Nakhon Phanom

At the end of Highway 22 on the banks of the Mekong River 242 kilometres (150 miles) east of Udon, this small town offers little of interest except its idyllic location. Across the river is a magnificent panorama of the mountains in Laos which are hauntingly beautiful in their irregular, fantastic shapes, reminiscent of the bizarre scenery of Guilin in China.

Although by no means the best of a poor bunch of hotels in town, the River Inn, on Soontorn Vichit Road, has the advantage of being right on the river and its very basic guest rooms have splendid views. Dinner can be taken on the riverside terrace (superb Thai home cooking), and there is an adjoining nightclub which seems to be Nakhon Phanom's hot spot.

That Phanom

Also on the Mekong, 54 kilometres (34 miles) south of Nakhon Phanom, this tiny settlement is the site of Issan's most revered religious monument, which gives the town its name.

Wat That Phanom is the second most sacred Buddhist shrine after That Luang in Vientiane for both the Lao and the Thai of the Northeast. The focus of interest is the *that* (pronounced 'tot'), a tall square-based reliquary with a decorative spire. It was originally built in around the ninth century and survived, albeit with several restorations, until 1975 when it collapsed after four days of heavy rain. It has subsequently been rebuilt by the Fine Arts Department.

About eight kilometres (five miles) north of That Phanom and seven kilometres (4.3 miles) west is the village of Renu Nakhon noted for its weaving industry and handful of shops selling *mutmee* cloth and embroidered clothing. There is also a *that* here, smaller than the one at That Phanom but rather more decorative.

Other Northeast Towns

Mukdahan

Another riverine town, 53 kilometres (33 miles) south of That Phanom. Mostly interesting for its location, although Wat Sri Nongkran, built by Vietnamese refugees in 1956, holds a certain fascination in its mix of Thai, Chinese and Vietnamese styles and motifs.

Ubon Ratchathani

A largish town, 160 kilometres (99 miles) south of Mukdahan, Ubon was an American air base during the Vietnam War. Today it has little to recommend it other than its annual Candle Festival, held on the full moon of the eighth lunar month (July) to celebrate the day of the Rains Retreat. This is a colourful pageant with a procession around town of floats bearing giant, intricately fashioned wax candles.

A worthwhile excursion from Ubon is to Khong Chiam, about 100 kilometres (65 miles) to the east at the point where the Mun River flows into the Mekong. The scenery here is quite spectacular.

Surin

Some 260 kilometres (162 miles) west of Ubon, towards Khorat, Surin is most famous as the site of the Elephant Round-Up held every year in November. Sponsored by the Tourism Authority of Thailand, this event is not in fact strictly a round-up, as all the elephants are already fully trained. But it is the one time when you can see such a large number of pachyderms all in one place. The people of Surin are renowned for their skill in elephant handling, and highlights of the round-up include a display of the elephant's ability as a work animal and a mock battle—the show's climax—with elephants dressed in the war regalia of olden times. Special tours by bus and train are operated from Bangkok at the time of the round-up.

From Surin it is roughly 200 kilometres (125 miles) back to Khorat.

Other Festivals

For anyone really captivated by the culture of the Northeast, two other festivals are worth noting.

The Rocket Festival Held throughout the Northeast in May, but most spectacularly seen in Yasothon, northwest of Ubon, the rocket festival derives from the tradition of calling upon celestial beings to send the rains in season and takes place immediately prior to rice planting. At Yasothon the event involves contests for the best decorated rocket and for the best performance when the rockets are fired on the following day.

The Wax Castle Ceremony Held at Sakhon Nakhon on the full moon of the 11th lunar month (October), this festival involves elaborate castles made from beeswax which are taken in procession and offered at various temples to make merit for ancestors. A boat race is held two days after the main ceremony.

Sacrificial Offerings

One of the less innocent superstitions, if you believe the missionary Bishop Bruguierie, is one that calls for human blood to be sprayed upon the foundation of all new gates constructed in the walls of the city. Modern travellers have confirmed the existence of this gruesome practice in Central Africa. In Siam, this custom is still very much alive today; a grisly tradition which has existed for centuries and which originated in an era of primitive barbarians, whose roots can be traced back to the Orient and Central Asia. The Bishop Pallegoix, while admitting to having seen something similar in the annals of Siam, would not confirm these facts to the extent that his colleague would, who tells the following story:

"When a new gate is to be constructed in the ramparts of the city, or when an existing one is to be repaired, then three innocent men must be sacrificed. This is how this barbaric execution is carried out: The king, after holding a secret council meeting, sends one of his officers to the place where the gate is to be constructed. This officer pretends to be calling out to someone, repeating the name that will be given to the new gate. After repeated calls, the passers-by, hearing his cry, turn to look; at that moment the officer, with the help of his assistants, stop three men at random. Their death is inevitable; no service, no promise, no sacrifice can save them. A pit is dug out of the door; above this hangs an enormous beam which is held up by two ropes and suspended horizontally, like those used in a wine press. On the fateful day, a splendid meal is give to the three ill-fated victims. They are then led to a ceremony at the tragic pit. The king and his court come to salute them. In private, the king assigns them the responsibility of guarding the gate that will confine them forever, and to not fail to give warning if enemies or rebels come to take the city. The moment that the ropes are cut, the unwitting martyrs are crushed under the heavy mass that falls on their heads. The Siamese believe that the men are transformed into spirits whom they call 'phi'. Peasants comment amongst themselves that this sanctioned homicide is necessary in order to establish guardians, so they say, of the treasure that lies within the walls of this city".

Henri Mouhot, Voyages dan les Royaumes de Siam (1868)
translated by Sarah Jessup

The Deep South

Southern Thailand is mostly visited for its beaches and islands, the top spots being Phuket, Koh Samui, and to a lesser extent Songkhla. The Deep South does, however, have some cultural and historical attractions. Like the North, the region was partly autonomous, in fact if not in theory, until the 20th century and so it presents some differences in lifestyles and customs. There are also topographic and climatic differences: most visibly, rubber plantations are rather more common than rice paddy fields.

The inland towns do offer opportunities for the traveller who likes to get off the beaten track. They can be easily combined with resort vacations. For example, after Koh Samui the traveller can head south from Surat Thani, or from Phuket cross the peninsula down to Hat Yai and then journey either north through Nakhon Si Thammarat to Surat Thani, or south to the Malaysian border.

The gateway to the Deep South is Surat Thani, which can be reached from Bangkok by domestic flight, overnight train or bus. The same applies to Hat Yai, the region's largest town not far from the Malaysian border. From Hat Yai there are flights to Surat Thani and Nakhon Si Thammarat, and to Pattani and Narathiwat. Domestic air services are also operated from Phuket to Surat Thani and Hat Yai. As in other parts of Thailand, local bus services connect all main towns in the region.

Surat Thani

Located on the Ta Pi River close to the coast 634 kilometres (395 miles) south of Bangkok, Surat Thani is a busy commercial centre and focal point for the local boat-building, fishing and mining industries. It has little to offer the visitor itself but is a base for an excursion to the historically important site of Chaiya, an hour to the north by train, less by road.

Chaiya is believed by some historians to have been the capital of the Srivijaya empire which held sway over the southern peninsula and Indonesian archipelago between the late seventh and 13th centuries. (Palembang in Sumatra is the other contender for the honour.)

The most important remaining monument from this period is **Wat Phra Boromathat**, just outside town. Most interesting are the cloister behind the *viharn* where there is a gallery containing a number of Buddha images, and the Javanese-style *prang*.

Nearby is a small museum (open Wednesday to Sunday 9 am – noon and 1–4 pm) housing a collection of mostly copies of the finest

Srivijaya sculpture, the originals now being in Bangkok's National Museum.

Other Chaiya monuments are **Wat Long**, where a brick *chedi* survives, **Wat Ratanaram**, and **Wat Keo** with the remains of a Srivijaya-style brick *prang*.

A short ride from Chaiya is the modern but equally fascinating **Wat Mok Khapalaram**, a temple and spiritual retreat set in a pleasantly wooded area. Such is its reputation that it attracts pilgrims from all over Thailand, while for the ordinary visitor it is remarkable for its collection of paintings on a variety of subjects executed by a wandering Zen Buddhist, Emmanuel Sherman.

Nakhon Si Thammarat

This historic city, 774 kilometres (481 miles) south of Bangkok and 140 kilometres (87 miles) south of Surat Thani, one of the oldest settlements in Thailand, was an important centre in the Dvaravati and Srivijaya kingdoms.

Nakhon Si Thammarat's most striking monument is **Wat Mahathat**, towards the southern side of town. Excavations have dated its foundations from the Srivijaya period and it thus ranks as one of Thailand's oldest temples. The compound is dominated by a 77-metre (245-foot) high *chedi* and the several temple buildings are worthy of study.

Next to Wat Mahathat is **Viharn Luang**, a much-restored building which nevertheless is a classic example of Ayutthaya period architectural style.

On the southern edge of town is the museum which has a small but fine collection of antiquities from the region, as well as some sculpture of Indian origin attesting to Nakhon Si Thammarat's early importance.

The town is also something of a crafts and cultural centre and is noted for its nielloware (this inlaid silverwork was first introduced to Thailand here), its shadow-play puppets and the *manora* dance drama.

Hat Yai

Hat Yai, located 947 kilometres (590 miles) south of Bangkok and 194 kilometres (120 miles) south of Nakhon Si Thammarat, is the south's main commercial centre and, because of its proximity to the border, it thrives on trade and tourism from Malaysia. The latter industry depends heavily on nightlife attractions, and bars, nightclubs and massage parlours abound. Shopping is also an important activity, though most of the items — fresh produce and imported goods — are largely aimed at the local market.

For the international traveller Hat Yai is really only notable for its bullfights, a sport traditional to the south and involving contests between bull and bull, not bull and man as in Spain. Again unlike the Hispanic version, the fight is not to the death.

South of Hat Yai the larger towns are Pattani, Yala and Narathiwat, from where the main road goes on to the Malaysian border. In this area the Muslim Malay influence becomes readily apparent.

Nature Reserves

For the nature lover the south boasts a number of splendid nature reserves, the two best being **Khao Chong** in Trang Province, a tropical rainforest with exceptional flora and fauna, and **Koh Tarutao National Park**, an island marine reserve off the west coast near the Malaysian border (to reach it, boats may be hired from Ban Pakbara, accessible from Hat Yai by bus).

Recommended Reading

Art

Boisselier, Jean. *The Heritage of Thai Sculpture*. (Weatherhill: 1974). A lavish and comprehensive book.

Boisselier, Jean. *Thai Painting*. (Tokyo: Kodansha International, 1976). Standard work on mural painting and the minor decorative arts such as gilt on lacquer.

Cadet, J.M. *Ramakien*. (Tokyo: Kodansha International, 1970). The *Ramakien* epic as told through the bas-reliefs at Bangkok's Wat Po.

Charoenwongse, Pisit and M.C. Subhadradis Diskul. *Thailand*. (In *Archaeologia Mundi* series. Geneva: Nagel, 1978). Good general study of architecture, sculpture and pottery in the various art periods.

Diskul, M.C. Subhadradis. *Art in Thailand: A Brief History*. (Bangkok: Silpakorn University, 1970). A useful introduction to the subject.

Hoskin, John. *Ten Contemporary Thai Artists*. (Bangkok: Eraphis, 1984). Profiles of ten leading painters.

Krairiksh, Piriya. *Art Styles in Thailand*. (Bangkok: 1977). An alternative and slightly controversial categorization of art styles and their periods.

Krairiksh, Piriya. *Art in Thailand Since 1932*. (Bangkok, 1983). A good, brief survey of contemporary painting and sculpture.

Le May, Reginald. *A Concise History of Buddhist Art in Thailand* (2nd Edition). (Tokyo, Charles Tuttle, 1963). Useful companion to other general surveys of Thai sculpture.

Muang Boran Publishing. *Mural Paintings of Thailand* series. (Bangkok). Separate volumes on the murals of individual temples.

Pawlin, Alfred. *Dhamma Vision*. (Bangkok: 1984). Buddhist-inspired paintings by a selection of the country's leading contemporary artists.

Stratton, Carol and Miriam McNair Scott. *The Art of Sukhothai*. (Kuala Lumpur: Oxford University Press, 1981). Handsome volume on the art of the first and perhaps most formative Thai period.

Van Beek, S and L. Invernizzi Tettoni. *The Arts of Thailand*. (Hong Kong: Travel Asia Publishing, 1985.) Excellent introduction to the subject accompanied by superb colour photographs.

Warren, William and Brian Brake. *The House on the Klong.* (Tokyo: Weatherhill). Illustrated book on the Jim Thompson House in Bangkok and its art collection.

Wray, Elizabeth et al. *Ten Lives of the Buddha.* (Tokyo: Weatherhill, 1972). The last ten and most important *Jataka* tales (previous lives of the Buddha) which provide the subject matter for many temple mural paintings.

Background Guides

Clarac, A and M. Smithies. *Guide to Thailand.* (Kuala Lumpur: Oxford University Press/DK Book House, 1981). The 'Baedeker' of Thailand with detailed descriptions of temples and historical sites throughout the country.

Various authors. *Thailand into the 80s.* (Bangkok: National Identity Office, 1984). Good general survey of the country, its people, economy, administration, etc.

Buddhism in Thailand

Bruce, Helen. *Nine Temples of Bangkok.* (Bangkok, Chalermnit). Interesting background on major Buddhist temples.

Dhani Nivat, Prince. *A History of Buddhism in Siam.* (Bangkok: Siam Society, 1965). Interesting general study.

Jumsai, M.L. Manich. *Understanding Thai Buddhism.* (Bangkok: Chalermnit). Somewhat idiosyncratic in style, but gives all the basic details.

Hilltribes

Lewis, Paul and Elaine. *Peoples of the Golden Triangle.* (London, Thames and Hudson, 1984). Probably the best and most comprehensive introduction to the various hilltribes who inhabit northern Thailand.

Media Transasia. *From the Hands of the Hills.* (Bangkok, 1978). Lavishly illustrated book dealing with hilltribe handicrafts.

History

Chakrabongse, Prince Chula. *Lords of Life.* (Bangkok: DD Books, reprint 1982). Individual portraits of the kings of the Chakri dynasty.

Coedes, G. *The Making of Southeast Asia.* (Berkeley and Los Angeles: University of California Press, 1966). Expert study of the founding and early development of the Indochinese states.

Collis, Maurice. *Siamese White*. (Bangkok, DD Books: reprint 1982). A thrilling adventure and reliable history of Samuel White, an Englishman in the employ of King Narai in the late 17th century.

Hall, D.G.E. *A History of Southeast Asia* (3rd Edition). (London: Macmillan, 1968). Standard history of the region.

Hutchinson, E.W. *Adventurers in Siam in the 17th Century*. (Bangkok: DD Books, reprint 1985). A good account of King Narai's dealings with the West and of foreigners in Thailand at the time, including the remarkable Constantine Phaulkon. Ideally read in conjunction with *Siamese White*.

Jumsai, M.L. Manich. *Popular History of Thailand*. (Bangkok: Chalermnit). A short potted history.

Syamananda, Rong. *A History of Thailand* (3rd Edition). (Bangkok: Chulalongkorn University, 1977). A brief and rather uncritical historical survey.

Wyatt, David K. *Thailand: A Short History*. (New Haven: Yale University Press, 1984). The latest and best account of the country's development from pre-Thai civilization up to the present day.

Historical Accounts and Reminiscences

Anonymous. *An Englishman's Siamese Journals 1890—1893*. (Bangkok: Siam Media International Books). A fascinating account of an English surveyor's travels in Thailand in the late 19th century.

Bock, Carl. *Temples and Elephants*. (Originally published in 1884 and now available in two reprint editions, one by Oxford University Press, Singapore, and the other by White Orchid Press, Bangkok). Especially interesting details of northern Thailand in the late 19th century.

Bowring, Sir John. *The Kingdom and People of Siam* (2 vols). (Kuala Lumpur: Oxford University Press/DK Book House 1977 reprint of 1857 first edition). Sir John Bowring was the envoy of Queen Victoria who successfully negotiated the first full treaty between Britain and Thailand in 1855. Although he did not stay long in the country, he drew on contemporary accounts for his book which stands as a standard work on the country in the mid-19th century.

Smith, Dr. Malcolm. *A Physician at the Court of Siam*. (London: 1947. Now reprinted by Oxford University Press, Singapore). A revealing picture of the life of the royal household in the reign of King Rama V by an English doctor appointed for several years as a court physician.

Wood, W.A.R. *A Consul in Paradise*. (London: Souvenir Press, 1965). One of the most lively and interesting of reminiscences by old-hand foreign residents.

Miscellaneous

Blofeld, John and Philip Jones Griffiths. *Bangkok*. (Amsterdam: Time-Life Books, The Great Cities series, 1979). One of the better 'coffee table' photobooks on the Thai capital.

Warren, William. *Jim Thompson: The Legendary American of Thailand*. (Boston: Houghton Mifflin, 1970). A fascinating account of the man who built up the Thai silk industry after World War II and then disappeared in Malaysia in 1967 under circumstances still unexplained. One of Asia's great unsolved mysteries.

Warren, William and Dean Barrett. *Images of Thailand*. (Hong Kong: Hong Kong Publishing Co, 1981). Around the country in words and photographs.

Note: the two best Bangkok bookshops specializing in books on Thailand and Southeast Asia are: Asia Books, 221 Sukhumvit Road, and DD Books, 32/9−10 Soi Asoke (21), Sukhumvit Road.

Thai Culture

Cooper, Robert and Nanthapa. *Culture Shock: Thailand*. (Singapore: Times Books International, 1982). Subtitled '. . . and how to survive it' and tells you how to avoid faux pas in the whole gamut of social intercourse.

Hollinger, Carol. *Mai Pen Rai*. (Boston: Houghton Mifflin, 1977). A humorous and most perceptive account of an expat's life in Bangkok in the late 1950s.

Mulder, Niels. *Everyday Life in Thailand*. (Bangkok: DK Books). Good account of Thai social values.

Seagaller, Dennis. *Thai Ways*. (Bangkok: 1980) and *More Thai Ways*. (Bangkok: 1982). Companion volumes that comprise a gold-mine of information and anecdotes about diverse aspects of Thai culture.

Major Thai Festivals and Holidays

Festivals are an essential part of Thai life. Many of them follow the lunar calendar and thus are 'moveable' feasts, while others have set annual dates. The following are the most important yearly celebrations.

January

New Year's Day — 1 January is an official Thai holiday.

February

Makha Bucha — Falling on the day of the full moon, this important Buddhist holiday commemorates the occasion when 1,250 disciples gathered spontaneously to hear the Buddha speak. The day of merit-making ends with candlelit processions around temples.

April

Chakri Day — 6 April is a national holiday to commemorate the founding of the Chakri Dynasty.

Songkran — 13 April marks the Thai New Year. Essentially a religious holiday when lustral water is sprinkled on Buddha images, it has become, especially in Chiang Mai, a time of good-natured highjinks involving throwing water over one and all.

May

Ploughing Ceremony — Takes place at the Pramane Ground in Bangkok at the beginning of the planting season on a date determined by Brahman priests. Presided over by His Majesty the King, the ceremony involves the ritual ploughing by sacred oxen and the planting of specially blessed rice seeds. A prediction is made for the success of the year's harvest.

Labour Day — 1 May is an official Thai holiday.

Coronation Day — 5 May commemorates the coronation of the present king.

Visakha Bucha — The most important date in the Buddhist calendar celebrating the day (in different years) on which the Buddha was born, achieved enlightenment and died. It falls on the day of the full moon and there are candlelit processions around temples in the evening.

July

Asanha Bucha — Falling on the day of the full moon, this is the anniversary of the Buddha's first sermon to his first five disciples. It marks the beginning of Buddhist

Lent, *Khao Phansa*, a three-month period of retreat for monks.

August

Queen's Birthday — 12 August is a public holiday to celebrate Her Majesty Queen Sirikit's birthday.

October

Ok Phansa — This holiday celebrates the Buddha's return to earth after spending one Lent season preaching in heaven. It also marks the end of the Lent period and the beginning of *Krathin*, the traditional time for presenting new robes and other gifts to monks at temples throughout the country.

Chulalongkorn Day — 23 October is the anniversary of the death of King Chulalongkorn, Rama V. Floral tributes and incense are placed at the foot of the monarch's equestrian statue in front of the old National Assembly building.

November

Loy Krathong — Held on the night of the full moon, this enchanting festival pays homage to Mae Khongkha, goddess of rivers and waterways. Throughout the country Thais gather by rivers, canals, lakes and ponds to float *krathongs*, colourful little lotus-shaped 'boats' bearing the traditional offerings of flowers, a candle, incense and a coin.

Golden Mount Fair — Bangkok's biggest temple fair held at Wat Saket by the Golden Mount.

Elephant Round-Up — An annual show in Surin featuring a large gathering of trained elephants which display work skills, perform games and parade in the battle regalia of old.

December

The King's Birthday — 5 December is the birthday of His Majesty King Bhumibol Adulyadej and is a public holiday.

Constitution Day — 10 December, a public holiday.

New Year's Eve — 31 December, a public holiday.

Note: if any major event falls on the weekend, the next working day is taken as the public holiday.

Practical Information

Basic Thai Vocabulary

Thai, like Chinese and other related languages and dialects in East and Southeast Asia, is a tonal, mostly monosyllabic language. This makes Thai particularly difficult for speakers of non-tonal languages (including speakers of European languages) to learn. Complicating the picture even further is the Thai alphabet, based on Devengari, an ancient south Indian script. And there is no standard romanization system, resulting in a variety of spellings for even common place names: Ayutthaya/Ayudhaya, Chiang Mai/Chieng-mai, Chao Phraya/Chao Phya, etc.

Below is a short list of the words and phrases most easily and usefully learned by the short-term visitor. Even the most mangled attempt to speak Thai is welcomed with friendly laughter and encouragement and is a good way to break the ice (and often bring down prices in shops and markets). For those who envision a more serious commitment to learning Thai, dictionaries and phrase books are widely available; the truly devoted should contact the American University Alumini Association (AUA), which runs a number of Thai- and English-language programmes throughout the country. (AUA, 179 Rajdamri Road, Bangkok; tel. 252-7069.)

Numbers

one	neung	หนึ่ง
two	sorng	สอง
three	sam	สาม
four	see	สี่
five	haa	ห้า
six	hok	หก
seven	jet	เจ็ด
eight	paet	แปด
nine	kao	เก้า
ten	sip	สิบ
eleven	sip-et	สิบเอ็ด
twelve	sip sorng	สิบสอง
fifteen	sip haa	สิบห้า
twenty	yee sip	ยี่สิบ
twenty-one	yee sip-et	ยี่สิบเอ็ด
twenty-two	yee sip sorng	ยี่สิบสอง
thirty	sam sip	สามสิบ
fifty	haa sip	ห้าสิบ
one hundred	neung roi	หนึ่งร้อย
one thousand	neung paen	หนึ่งพัน
ten thousand	neung meun	หนึ่งหมื่น
one hundred thousand	neung saen	หนึ่งแสน
one million	neung laan	หนึ่งล้าน

Basic Phrases

thank you	khawp khun khrap (male)	ขอบคุณครับ
	khawp khun khaa (female)	ขอบคุณค่ะ
hello, goodbye	sawat dee (khrap or khaa)	สวัสดีค่ะ หรือ ครับ
excuse me	khor thot	ขอโทษ
never mind	mai pen rai	ไม่เป็นไร
no	mai	ไม่
yes	chai (it is) or simply	ใช่, ครับ หรือ ค่ะ
	'khrap' or 'kha'	
how are you?	sabai dee reu?	สบายดีเหรอ
I'm fine	sabai dee (khrap . . .)	สบายดี (ครับ หรือ ค่ะ)
I don't feel well	mai sabai (khrap . . .)	ไม่สบาย

Questions and Directions

what is your name?	khun cheu arai khrap?	คุณชื่ออะไรครับ
my name is . . .	phom (male) chun	ผมชื่อ (ผู้ชาย), ฉันชื่อ (ผู้หญิง)
	(female) cheu . . .	
where is . . .	you nai?	อยู่ไหน
I want to go to . . .	yaak ja pai . . .	อยากจะไป
turn left	leou sai	เลี้ยวซ้าย
turn right	leou khwa	เลี้ยวขวา
straight ahead	trong pai	ตรงไป
stop here	yoot tee nee	หยุดที่นี่
how much does this cost?	nee baht taw rai?	นี่บาทเท่าไหร่

Places

hotel	rawng ram	โรงแรม
street	tanon	ถนน
side street	soi	ซอย
bus station	sat-hani rot meh	สถานีรถเมล์
railway station	sat-hani rot fai	สถานีรถไฟ
airport	sanam bin (in Bangkok 'Don Muang')	สนามบิน (ในกรุงเทพ เรียก "ดอนเมือง")
city	nakhon	นคร
town	muang	เมือง
village	ban	บ้าน
beach	haat	หาด
island	koh	เกาะ
mountain, hill	doi, khao	เขา, ดอย
restaurant	raan ahaan	ร้านอาหาร
hospital	rong phaya-bahn	โรงพยาบาล
post office	prai-sannee	ไปรษณีย์
police station	sat-hani tamruat	สถานีตำรวจ
embassy	sat-han toot	สถานทูต
bathroom	hawng nam	ห้องน้ำ
room	hawng	ห้อง
market	talatt	ตลาด
river	menam	แม่น้ำ
nation	prahtett	ประเทศ

Useful Words

today	wan nee	วันนี้
yesterday	meua wan nee	เมื่อวานนี้
tomorrow	proong nee	พรุ่งนี้
day	wan	วัน
week	ahtit	อาทิตย์
month	deun	เดือน
year	pee	ปี
hungry	hew kao	หิวข้าว
thirsty	hew nam	หิวน้ำ
food	ahahn	อาหาร
water	nam	น้ำ
train	rot fai	รถไฟ
auto	rot yon	รถยนต์
boat	reua	เรือ
airplane	kreung bin	เครื่องบิน
taxi	taksee	แท็กซี่

Food

water	nam	น้ำ
salt	kreua	เกลือ
sugar, sweet	wan	น้ำตาล, หวาน
chilli pepper	plik	พริก
beef	neua	เนื้อ
pork	moo	หมู
chicken	gai	ไก่
eggs	kai	ไข่
fish	plaa	ปลา
vegetables	pahk	ผัก
fruit	pohlamai	ผลไม้
rice	khao	ข้าว
to eat	khao	ทานข้าว
to drink	deum	ดื่ม
soup	tom	ต้ม
coffee	cafe	กาแฟ
tea	cha	ชา

Glossary

Apsara A female celestial dancer.

Bo or **Bodhi tree** The tree beneath which the Buddha meditated and attained Enlightenment.

Bodhisattva A saint in Mahayana Buddhism. In Theravada Buddhism it refers to the future Buddha in his previous incarnations.

Bot (also **Ubosot**) The ordination hall of a *wat*, architecturally similar to a *viharn*.

Brahma The four-faced 'Creator' in the Hindu trinity of principal gods.

Brahmanism The ancient religion of India, the forerunner of Hinduism and Buddhism. In Thailand the faith is closely allied with Buddhism and is practised by a small community of Brahman priests.

Chedi A solid monument, usually with a pointed spire, built to enshrine relics of the Buddha or those of his disciples, or to contain the ashes of important persons.

Chofa A slender, curved decoration, shaped rather like a swan's neck, adorning each end of the ridge of a *bot*'s or *viharn*'s roof. Possibly meant to symbolize the *garuda*.

Dhamma The law or teaching as preached by the Buddha.

Dhammachakra The 'Wheel of the Law' symbolizing the Buddha's teaching. The circular motif is commonly found in sculpture of the Dvaravati period.

Erawan Mythical three-headed white elephant, the mount of the god Indra.

Ganesha Elephant-headed Hindu god of literature and success.

Garuda Mythical king of the birds and mount of Vishnu. Often depicted as having a human torso and hands. It is the half-brother of the *naga* (king of serpents) and is its great enemy, frequently depicted clutching or fighting with a snake.

Hanuman A mythical monkey warrior who leads an army against the evil Toksakan in the *Ramakien* epic.

Indra Chief god of the heaven of 33 gods on top of Mount Meru.

Jataka The previous lives of the Buddha of which there are 550, although the last ten are the most important.

Khon Classical Thai dance drama form in which masks are worn. The narrative content is taken from the *Ramakien* epic.

Kinnari A mythical creature, half-bird and half-woman.

Mahayana Buddhism Also known as the 'Greater Vehicle', and one of the two principal Buddhist sects. Its main tenet is that those who have achieved enlightenment should refrain from entering nirvana and instead remain to assist others (the ideal of the *bodhisattva*). Such sects as Zen and Nichiren belong to the Mahayana Buddhist tradition.

Mara The force of evil which tempted the Buddha to give up his aim of achieving enlightenment in return for all the earthly delights.

Meru The mythical mountain abode of the gods. Symbolized by the *prang* in Khmer and Lopburi architecture.

Mondop A square building housing a Buddha image or other sacred object.

Mudra A hand gesture of the Buddha.

Naga Mythical king of the serpents and half-brother of the *garuda*, its sworn enemy.

Nirvana The state of the extinction of suffering which is reached after enlightenment has been attained and one is released from the cycle of death and rebirth.

Pali The scriptural language derived from Sanskrit and in which Theravada Buddhist texts are written.

Prang A tall finger-like spire, usually richly carved. Originally a common feature in Khmer architecture and later adopted by Thai builders.

Prasat A tower sanctuary in Khmer architecture. In Thai architecture it is a royal religious edifice, usually of a cruciform pattern and topped by a *prang*.

Ramakien The Thai version of the Indian *Ramayana* epic which recounts the story of Rama and the rescue of his wife, Sita, from the clutches of Totsakan, King of the Demons.

Sala A small open-sided pavilion used as a meeting or resting place. Often found in temple compounds and frequently built over or by a body of water.

Sema A stone slab placed at the corners and axes of *bot*.

Siva 'The Destroyer' in the Hindu trinity of the principal gods.

Stupa Synonymous with *chedi*.

That A northeastern (originally Lao) form of reliquary tower with a square base and decorative spire.

Theravada Buddhism The 'Doctrine of the Elders' sometimes called 'Hinayana' or 'Lesser Vehicle', practised in Thailand, Laos, Kampuchea, Burma, Sri Lanka and India.

Viharn Main hall of a temple used for day-to-day services.

Wat Describes an entire temple compound. The word means both 'temple' and 'monastery'.

Useful Addresses

Bangkok

Local directory assistance	tel. 13
Domestic long distance information	tel: 101
International directory assistance	tel. 100
Police (Special Tourist Branch)	tel. 221-6206/10
Ambulance	tel. 281-1544,199
Fire	tel. 252-2171/5
Central Post Office	tel. 233-1050
New Road	
Immigration	tel. 286-4233, 286-4231
South Sathorn Road	
Railway Station (Hualampong)	tel. 223-7461, 233-0341/8
International Airport Information	tel. 535-1111, 535-1254
Domestic Airport	tel. 535-2081/6
American Express Office	tel. 251-4914, 236-0276
4th Floor Siam Center	
965 Rama I Road	
Eastern Bus Terminal	tel. 391-2504
North/Northeastern Bus Terminal	tel. 271-0101/5
Southern Bus Terminal	tel. 411-4978/9

Airlines

Air France	tel. 233-9477, 234-1333
G/fl, Charn Issara Tower,	
942/51 Rama IV Road	
Air India	tel. 256-9614/19
16/fl, Amarin Plaza,	
500 Ploenchit Road	
Air Lanka	tel. 236-9292/3, 236-4981
G/fl, Charn Issara Tower,	
942/34-35 Rama IV Road	
British Airways	tel. 236-0038
2/fl Charn Issara Tower	
Rama IV Road	
Burma Airways	tel. 234-9692
208 Surawong Road	

Cathay Pacific Airways 5/fl Charn Issara Tower 942/136 Rama IV Road	tel. 237-6161, 235-4330, 233-6105
China Airlines 4/fl, Peninsula Plaza 153 Rajadamri Road	tel. 253-4241/4, 253-4438
Garuda 944/19 Rama IV Road	tel. 233-3873, 233-0981/2
C.A.A.C. 134/1-2 Rama IV Road	tel. 235-6510/1, 235-1880/2
Japan Airlines M Floor Wall Street Tower 33–34 Surawong Road	tel. 233-2440, 234-9111
KLM Royal Dutch Airlines 2 Patpong Road	tel. 235-5150/9
Korean Airlines Dusit Thani Hotel, Rama IV Road	tel. 234-9283/9
Lufthansa German Airlines 1 Floor, 2/2 Wireless Road	tel. 255-0370/1
Malaysian Airlines System 98/102 Surawong Road	tel. 236-4705/9
Philippine Airlines 1–3/fl Charn Issara Tower Rama IV Road	tel. 233-2350/2
Qantas Airways Charn Issara Tower 942/51 Rama IV Road	tel. 236-9193/5, 236-0102
Royal Nepal Airlines 1/4 Convent Road	tel. 233-3921/4
SAS Scandinavian Airlines System 412 Rama I Road	tel. 253-8333, 253-8444
Singapore Airlines 2 Silom Road	tel. 236-0303, 236-0440
Swissair Transport 1 Silom Road	tel. 233-2935/9
Thai Airways Co. Ltd. (Domestic)	tel. 280-0080, 280-0090
Thai Airways International 485 Silom Road	tel. 233-3810, 234-3100

Banks

Bank of Thailand Bangkhunprom	tel. 282-3322
Bangkok Bank 333 Silom Road	tel. 234-3333
Bank of America 2/2 Witthayu Road	tel. 251-6333/67
Chase Manhattan Bank 965 Rama I Road, Siam Center	tel. 252-1141
Hongkong and Shanghai Bank 64 Silom Road	tel. 233-5996
Standard Chartered Bank Saladaeng Circle, Rama IV Road	tel. 234-0821

Churches

Holy Redeemer Church (Roman Catholic) 123/19 Soi Ruam Rudee	tel. 252-5097
Calvary Baptist Church Soi 2 Sukhumvit Road	tel. 251-8278
Christ Church (Anglican/Episcopal) Convent Road	tel. 234-3634

Department Stores

Central Department Store 306 Silom Road	tel. 233-6930/9
Robinson Department Store 2 Silom Road	tel. 235-6690
Sogo Department Store Amarin Plaza, Ploenchit Road	tel. 256-9131

Embassies

Australia 37 Sathorn Tai Road	tel. 287-2680
Myanmar (formerly Burma) 132 Sathorn Nua Road	tel. 234-4698

Canada 11th Floor, Boonmitr Building 138 Silom Road	tel. 234-1561/8
China 57 Ratchadaphisek Road	tel. 245-7032, 245-7037/8
France Customs House Lane	tel. 234-0950
Germany 9 Sathorn Tai Road	tel. 213-2331/6, 286-9006
India 4-6 Soi Prasanmit, Sukhumvit Road	tel. 258-0300/6
Indonesia 600–2 Phetburi Road	tel. 252-3135/40
Italy 399 Nang Linchi Road	tel. 287-2054/7
Japan 1674 New Phetburi Road	tel. 252-6151/9
Malaysia 35 Sathorn Tai Road	tel. 286-1390/2
Nepal 189 Sukhumvit Road Soi 71	tel. 391-7240
Netherlands 106 Wireless Road	tel. 254-7701/5
New Zealand 93 Wireless Road	tel. 251-8165
Philippines 760 Sukhumvit Road	tel. 259-0140
Singapore 129 Sathorn Tai Road	tel. 286-2111, 286-1434
Sweden 11th Floor Boonmitr Building 138 Silom Road	tel. 234-3891
United Kingdom 1031 Wireless Road	tel. 253-0191/9
United States 95 Wireless Road	tel. 252-5040/9
USSR 108 Sathorn Nua Road	tel. 234-9824, 235-5599

Hospitals

Bumrungrad Medical Center 33 Soi Nananua (3) Sukhumvit	tel. 253-0250/9 emergency 251-0415
Saint Louis Hospital 215 Sathorn Tai Road	tel. 212-0033/48
Samitivej Hospital 133 Soi Klang(49) Sukhumvit	tel. 392-0011/9
Bangkok Adventist Hospital 430 Pisanuloke Road	tel. 281-1422, 282-1100

Rental Car Agencies

Avis Car Rental 981 Silom Road	tel. 233-0397
Thongchai Car Rental 1448/1 New Phetburi Road	tel. 253-7678/9

Tourist Authority of Thailand (T.A.T.) by City

Bangkok (Head Office) Rajadamnoen Nok Avenue	tel. 282-1143/5/7
Chiang Mai 135 Paisanee Road (Area Code 053)	tel. 235-334
Hat Yai Thanon Soi 2, Nipat-Utit 3	tel. 243-747, 245-986 (Area Code 074)
Kanchanaburi Saengshotto Road	tel. 511-200 (Area Code 034)
Nakhon Ratchasima (Khorat) 53/1-4 Mukmontri Road	tel. 243-427, 243-751 (Area Code 044)
Pattaya 382/1 Chaihaad Road, Moo 10, Banglamoong	tel. 428-750, 249-113 (Area code 038)
Phitsanulok 209/7-8 Surasi Shopping Center Boromtrailoknart Road	tel. 252-742, 252-743 (Area Code 055)
Phuket 73-5 Phuket Road, Phuket Town	tel. 212-213, 211-036 (Area Code 076)
Surat Thani Sala Prachakom, Na Muang Road	tel. 282-828 (Area Code 077)

Hotels

Thailand boasts some of the finest hotel accommodation in the world, with service to match. What's more, some of the best gourmet food to be had anywhere in Thailand is featured in Bangkok's finer hotel restaurants.

Every town of moderate size or larger has at least one hotel offering standard accommodation or better. Inexpensive but comfortable guesthouses make Thailand a popular destination among budget travellers as well. Luxury hotel bills are subject to a 10–25 percent tax surcharge.

Price Rating System:	*	Budget, less than B1000/night
	**	Moderate, B1000-2000/night
	***	Expensive, B2000-3500/night
	****	Luxury, over B3500/night

Bangkok

Luxury and First-Class Hotels

Airport Hotel 333 Chert Wudthakas Road tel. 566-1020	***	300 rooms. Convenient for a one-night stopover in Bangkok.
Ambassador Hotel 8 Sukhumvit Road Soi 11 tel. 254-0444	***	935 rooms in three different wings: Chavalit wing (cheapest), Ambassador wing and the luxury Tower wing. One of the best bargains in town.
Central Plaza Hotel 1695 Phaholyothin Road tel. 541-1234	***	607 rooms. Located about 15 kilometres (nine miles) from downtown Bangkok. Popular for conventions.
Dusit Thani Hotel Rama IV Road– Silom Road tel. 236-0450/9	****	525 rooms. Long-established, top hotel with some huge guest rooms and seven restaurants.
Hilton International 2 Wireless Road tel. 253-0123	***	343 rooms. A Bangkok landmark. Noted for its beautiful gardens and fine rooms.

Holiday Inn Crowne Plaza 981 Silom Road tel. 238-4300, 254-0023	***	385 rooms. Business centre, swimming pool and shopping arcade.
Imperial Hotel Wireless Road tel. 254-0111	***	400 rooms. Tennis courts. Popular for conventioners. Big discounts for business.
The Menam Hotel 2074 New Road Yannawa tel. 289-1148/9, 289-0352/3	***	727 rooms. On the river; also newly opened. Tennis courts, jogging track. Suites up to B15,000 per night.
Montien Hotel 54 Surawong Road tel. 234-8060/9	***	435 rooms. Located in the heart of Bangkok's entertainment district.
Narai Hotel 222 Silom Road tel. 237-0100/39	**	500 rooms. Popular with Thais for its penthouse restaurant and lively disco.
Oriental Hotel 48 Oriental Avenue Bangkok 10500 tel. 236-0400	****	394 rooms. One of the finest hotels in the world and Bangkok's most expensive. On the river-front Superb food and room service.
The Regent of Bangkok 155 Rajdamri Road tel. 251-6127, 251-6370	****	400 rooms. Beautiful layout. Well- known for its food. Convenient if unattractive location.
Rose Garden Hotel and Country Resort 32 Petkasem Road Nakkon Pathom tel. 253-0295/7	**	120 rooms. Golf, tennis, bowling, swimming, gardens, dancing etc. Located about 30 kilometres (19 miles) west of Bangkok.
Royal Orchid Sheraton 2 Capt. Bush Lane Siphaya Road tel. 234-5599	***	776 rooms. On the river.
Shangri-La Hotel 89 Soi Wat Suan Plu tel. 236-7777	****	700 rooms. Excellent location on the river with exceptional lobby views.

Siam Intercontinental Rama I Road tel. 253-0355	****	400 rooms. Fantastic piece of architecture. Tennis courts, mini zoo. Very popular hotel.
Tawana Ramada 80 Surawong Road tel. 236-0361	***	265 rooms. Located on a busy street.

Standard Accommodation

Federal Hotel 27 Soi 11 Sukhumvit tel. 253-0175	*	93 rooms. Good budget accommodation. One of the many Vietnam-era hotels built for the American GIs on 'R & R'.
Impala Hotel 9 Soi 24 Sukhumvit Road tel. 259-0053/4	**	220 rooms. Good value. 24-hour coffee shop features jazz some evenings.
Manhattan Hotel 12 Soi 15 Sukhumvit Road tel. 255-0166, 255-0188	**	200 rooms. Comfortable family-style hotel.
New Trocadero Hotel 343 Surawong Road tel. 234-8920/9	**	131 rooms. Located near New Road and Chinatown.
Royal Hotel 2 Rajdamnoen Avenue tel. 222-9111/7	**	297 rooms. Close to the palace and temple complexes of Sanum Luang.
The Mermaid's Rest 6/1 Sukhumvit, Soi 8 tel. 253-3548	*	190 rooms. Lovely garden and pool. One of the best value hotels in Bangkok.

Budget Hotels and Guesthouses

Grand Tower Guest House Soi 53 (Tong-Lor) Sukhumvit tel. 259-0380	**	104 rooms for short-term visitors. All rooms carpeted, air-conditioned, hot and cold water. One of the best swimming pools in town.

Swan Hotel 31 Custom House Lane New Road tel. 234-8594, 234-5198	*	72 rooms. Excellent value. However, rooms vary in quality and should be seen first.

Chantaburi

Eastern Hotel 899 Tha-chalaep Road	**	142 rooms. Swimming pool, night-club, coffee shop.

Chiang Mai

Chiang Inn Chiang Mai Hotel 100 Changkhlan road tel. 270-070/6	***	170 rooms. Downtown location. Nightclub, conference hall.
Chiang Mai Guest House 91 Charoen Prated Road tel. 236-501	*	29 rooms. Situated on the banks of the Ping River. Nice garden restaurant. Some rooms with airconditioning.
Chiang Mai Orchid Hotel 100-2 Huai Kaeo Road tel. 222-099	**	265 rooms. Very upmarket with a swimming pool, disco, conference facilities, etc.
Chiang Mai President Hotel 226 Witchayanon Road tel. 251-025	**	242 rooms. Conference facilities.
Dusit Inn 112 Changkhlan Road tel. 236-0450, 233-1140	**	200 rooms. Conference room, central location.
Isra Guest House Off Huai Kaeo Road tel. 214-924	*	12 rooms. Clean and comfortable. Bikes provided free of charge.
Je T'aime Guest House 247-9 Charoen Rat Road tel. 241-912	*	24 rooms. A famous and popular guesthouse for travellers.

Mae-Sa Valley Hill Resort Hotel c/o North West Tours in Suriwong Hotel tel. 236-789, 236-733	**	30 bungalows. Fine country resort.
Dusit Inn 112 Changkhlan Road	**	200 rooms. Conference room, central location.
Isra Guest House Off Huai Kaeo Road tel. 214-924	*	12 rooms. Clean and comfortable. Bikes provided free of charge.
Je T'aime Guest House 24-7 Charoen Rat Road tel. 241-912	*	24 rooms. A famous and popular guesthouse for travellers.
Porn-Ping Hotel 46-8 Charoenprathet Road tel. 270-099	**	180 rooms. Downtown. Conference room.
Poy Luang Hotel 146 Superhighway tel. 242-633	**	228 rooms. Out of town on the ring road. Revolving restaurant. Swimming pool.
Prince Hotel 3 Taiwan Road tel. 236-396	*	112 rooms. A popular, moderately priced hotel. Central location. Swimming pool.
Rincome Hotel 301 Huai Kaeo Road tel. 221-044, 221-130	**	158 rooms. On the road to Doi Suthep. Swimming pool best in town.
Riverview Lodge 25 Charoen Prattret, Soi 2 tel. 271-109/10	**	36 rooms, air-conditioned, over- looking the Ping River.
Suriwong Hotel 110 Changkhlan tel. 235-099	*	170 rooms. Downtown. Conference rooms.

Chiang Rai

Wiang Inn **
893 Phaholyothin Road
tel. 711-543, 711-533

260 rooms. Swimming pool,
shopping arcade, restaurant,
conference rooms.

Wangcome Hotel **
869/96 Pemaviphat Road
tel. 711-800, 711-811

221 rooms. A first-class hotel.
Restaurant etc.

Chiang Saen

Chiang-Saen Guest House *
45 Mekong Riverside

Pleasant lodging in a pleasant
town.

Hat Yai

Lee Gardens Hotel **
1 Lee Pattana Road
tel. 245-888, 245-884

122 rooms. Convention room,
restaurant, coffee shop, nightclub.

The Rama President Hotel *
420 Petchkasem Road
tel. 244-477, 244-921
tel. 579-5400 (Bangkok)

Rooms with fan and private bath.
Not bad for the price.

Hua Hin and Cha-Am

Hotel Sofitel Central ***
Damnoen Kase Road
tel. 512-021/40

A hotel 'with a history'. Formerly
the Railway Hotel. It has been
renovated to restore its old
colonial style. On the beach.

Royal Garden Resorts **
107/1 Petkasem Road
Hua Hin
tel. 511-881/4
tel. 252-4638 (Bangkok)

177 rooms. A top beach resort
suited for the family. Tennis, golf,
disco, rooftop cocktail terrace, etc.

The Regent Cha-Am **
849-21 Cha-Am Beach
tel. 251-0305
tel. 252-8319 (Bangkok)

362 rooms. Good family-style
beach resort. Tennis, squash, golf,
diving, etc.

Kanchanaburi

Rama of River **
Kwai Hotel
284/3-16 Saeng Chuto Road
River Kwai Village Hotel **
74 Ban Phutakhian
Sai Yok
tel. 251-755
tel. 251-7552, 251-7828 (Bangkok)

131 rooms. Pleasant staff, swimming pool. Only two kilometres (1.3 miles) to the 60 rooms. Reservations must be made in advance from Bangkok.

Khon Kaen

Kosa Hotel (Rama **
of Khon Kaen)
250-2 Srichan Road
tel. 236-771, 236-014

120 rooms. Very comfortable. Swimming pool, near disco, bowling alley, massage etc.

Koh Samui

Coral Bay Resort **
Chaweng Beach
Yai Noi Bay
tel. 272-222, 272-313
tel. 233-7711, 234-8141 (Bangkok)

42 bungalows, with fans and airconditioning, large seaview balconies.

Samui Yacht Club ***
Chaweng Beach
Tong Ta Kiam Bay
tel. 421-378
tel: 319-6042/3 (Bangkok)

40 luxurious Thai-style cottages set in tropical gardens on prime beach front.

Seafan Beach Resort ***
Maenam Beach
tel. 421-360
tel: 235-1017/8 (Bangkok)
Mae Hong Son

Comfortable lodgings with complete resort facilities, located on quiet beach.

Mae Tee Hotel *
55 Khunrum
Prapas Road
tel. 611-139

38 rooms some airconditioned. Best bet in town.

Mae Hong Son Resort	**	40 rooms with fans and air-conditioning.
24 Ban Huay Dua		
tel. 611-406		

Nakhon Phanom

The River Hotel	*	30 rooms. A bit run-down but charming atmosphere with a truly gourmet terrace restaurant. Air-conditioned rooms, nightclub. Views of Laos.
On the Mekong River		

Nakhon Si Thammarat

Thai Hotel	*	150 rooms. Restaurant, coffee shop, cocktail lounge.
1369-75 Rajadamnoen Road		
tel. 356-451, 356-505		

Pattaya

Asia Pattaya Hotel	**	320 rooms. Off the road to Montien Beach. Nice location.
Pattaya		
tel. 428-602/6		
tel. 215-0808 (Bangkok)		

Merlin Pattaya Hotel	**	360 rooms. Swimming pool, tennis courts etc.
Pattaya Beach Resort		
tel. 428-755/9		
tel. 233-0802 (Bangkok)		

Montien Pattaya Hotel	***	320 rooms. Several restaurants. Tennis courts, tour counter, etc.
Pattaya Beach Resort		
tel. 428-155/6		
tel. 233-7060 (Bangkok)		

Nipa Lodge	**	150 rooms. One of the first luxury hotels of Pattaya, still very popular.
Pattaya Beach Resort		
tel. 428-195, 428-321		
tel. 252-6118 (Bangkok)		

Ocean View Hotel	**	115 rooms. Beer garden, aviary.
Pattaya Beach Resort		
tel. 428-084, 428-434		
tel. 233-9755/9 (Bangkok)		

Orchid Lodge Pattaya Beach Resort tel. 428-161, 428-323 tel. 252-6045 (Bangkok)	**	243 rooms. Mini-golf course.
Pattaya 12 Soi 12 Pattaya Beach Road tel. 428-425, 429-239	*	One of the best budget hotels in town.
Royal Cliff Beach Hotel Pattaya Beach Resort tel. 421-421/30 tel. 282-0294 (Bangkok)	****	700 rooms. Pattaya's most luxurious hotel.
Royal Garden Hotel Banglamung 218 Pattaya Road tel. 428-126/7 tel. 460-1801/5 (Bangkok)	**	210 rooms. Tennis courts, shopping arcades.
Siam Bayshore Hotel Pattaya Beach Resort tel. 423-871/7 tel. 251-2458 (Bangkok)	**	275 rooms. Tennis courts, night-club.
Thanaporn Beach Cliff Hotel Banglamung Pattaya tel. 428-690	*	100 rooms. Next to the Asia Pattaya Hotel. Nice beach.
The Weekender Soi 2 Beach Road Pattaya tel. 428-720, 429-461	*	120 rooms. In town, good value.

Phitsanulok

Rajapruk Hotel 99/9 Phra-Ong Dam Road tel. 258-477 tel. 233-5727 (Bangkok)	*	100 rooms. Swimming pool, night club, banquet room, coffee shop.

Phuket

Coral Beach Hotel Patong Beach 104 Mu 4, Patong Beach Road tel. 321-106/12 tel. 252-6045 (Bangkok)	***	Located at the end of Patong Beach, with sweeping ocean views and good for families.
Kata Thani Hotel Kata Beach tel. 381-417/25 tel. 235-5120/4 (Bangkok)	***	Small hotel with cosy accommodations, beach front location, good for families.
Merlin Hotel Phuket Town 158/1 Yaowarat tel. 212-860/70 tel. 253-2536 (Bangkok)	**	Well-managed international hotel conveniently located in town.
Le Meridien Karon Noi Beach tel. 321-480/5 tel. 254-8147/50 (Bangkok)	****	Private beach, two pools, squash and tennis courts, luxurious facilities.
Patong Beach Hotel Patong Beach Thawiwong Road tel. 321-301/2, 321-304/5 tel. 233-0420, 233-2692 (Bangkok)	**	One of Patong's oldest hotels, set in a coconut grove near the beach.
Pearl Hotel Phuket Town 42 Montri Road tel. 311-338, 311-376/83 tel. 260 1022/6 (Bangkok)	**	Chinese decor, pleasant ambeance. Good service.
Phuket Arcadia Hotel Karon Beach tel. 381-433/41, 381-039/44 tel. 254-0921/2, 254-7091/2 (Bangkok)	****	Luxurious accommodation with extensive entertainment and sports facilities, including a 25-metre pool.

Phuket Yacht Club   ****   Very exclusive resort—expensive.
Nai Han Beach   A favourite of the international
23/3 Wiset Road   jet-set.
tel. 381-156/63
tel. 251-4707 (Bangkok)

Royal Park Beach Resort   ***   One of Phuket's newest resorts,
Bang Tao Bay   located on a private beach on the
Mu 2, Thambon Cheng Talay   sunset side of the island.
tel. 311-453, 311-409

Safari Beach Hotel   **   Modern accommodation with
Patong Beach   standard amenities, 16 km (10
83/12 Thawiwong Road   miles) from Phuket Town.
tel. 321-230/1
tel. 294-2723/5, 294-2732/6 (Bangkok)

South Sea Resort   **   200 rooms, each with a balcony
Karon Beach   and seaview. Mediterranean style
36/2, Mu 1, Liab Hadd Road   decor.
tel. 381-611/7
tel. 254-4971/2, 252-1264 (Bangkok)

Songkhla

Samila Hotel   **   70 rooms. On the beach and near a
Ratchadamnoen Road   golf-course.
Samila Beach
tel. 331310/4
tel. 281-6467 (Bangkok)

Surat Thani

Wang Tai Hotel   **   238 rooms. Mini-golf, restaurant,
1 Talat Mai Road   barber, coffee shop etc.
tel. 272-022
tel. 215-7801 (Bangkok)

Surin

Petchkasem Hotel   *
104 Jitburmrung Road
tel. 511-274, 511-576

162 rooms. Restaurant, meeting rooms.

Tak

Viang Tak Hotel   *
25/3 Mahatthai Bamrung Road
Bamrung Road
tel. 511-910
tel. 233-2690 (Bangkok)

100 rooms. Golf course and and boating facilities nearby. Nightclub and conference hall.

Ubon Ratchathani

Pathumrat Hotel   *
173 Chayang-kui Road
tel. 254-417, 254-547

120 rooms. Restaurant, nightclub, coffee shop.

Udon Thani

Charoen Hotel   *
549 Pho Sri Road
tel. 211-311

120 rooms. Best accommodation in Udon. Coffee shop, nightclub and function room.

Times around the World

When it's 12 noon in Bangkok (standard time for all of Thailand), the standard time in the following cities is:

Beijing	1 pm	Chicago	11 pm*
Hong Kong	1 pm	Honolulu	5 pm*
London	5 am	Los Angeles	9 pm*
New York	midnight*	Paris	6 am
San Francisco	9 pm*	Sydney	3 pm
Taipei	1 pm	Tokyo	2 pm

* On the preceding day.

The Rules of the Game

I first met Lek in a fifth-grade massage parlour. The place is tucked away in a little lane in Suriwong, the centre of the business world of Bangkok. Lek worked as a "bonded girl" there. The agent who brought Lek to Bangkok had lent her parents 1,500 baht on the condition that Lek came to work in Bangkok to pay off the debt. She had arrived a few weeks before I talked to her. She was plump and not at all good-looking, but she had a smiling and friendly face. She still had the look of a little girl and her figure was not fully developed. She did not appear to be miserable, as she was smiling all the time while we were talking. When asked if she liked the job, she said she did not. She would like to go home. When asked when she could go home, she said she did not know. Perhaps she would go home when she paid off the debt. As to the question when did she think she would work off the debt, the reply was she did not know. She could free herself if she could repay the loan of 1,500 baht by entertaining her customers. Since she got 10 baht per hour/customer, she would have to entertain at least 150 customers or work there 150 hours in order to work off her debts. However, she said that only a week ago her parents had come to ask her employer for an advance on her wage of another 1,500 baht. So this means that she had to stay longer in this place before she could be free, and she did not know when her freedom could be regained.

All her life Lek had known only poverty and hardship. She had seen some of the girls in the villages who had gone to Chiang Mai and Bangkok and had come back in their modern clothes looking very pretty and cheerful. She would like to go away and earn more cash to buy some of these nice clothes and have more money to buy food. In early 1980, an agent who had learnt about Lek's poverty and the family's plight came to see her parents and offered a loan of money if they would agree to send Lek to work in Cholburi. But initially, the agent only paid the parents a portion of 1,500 baht. Lek was not pretty and he was not assured of the income she would bring.

After a few months had passed, the parents wanted the other half of the money. The agent did not want to pay, so the parents went to report to the village headman that their daughter had been abducted. The deputy village headman went to see the agent and asked him to bring the girl back or else he would bring the police. The agent then brought Lek back to the village. This time another deal was made. The agent would pay the rest of the money but Lek had to go to Bangkok to work as she had not really worked off the debt. Obviously the agent had made another deal with the massage parlour in Bangkok for a larger sum of money and saw this as a chance to make more cash for himself. The father insisted that he would go to Bangkok to make sure that their daughter was in a good place. He was paid the other half of the loan and returned home.

Lek's story is not uncommon. The receptionist in Lek's massage parlour told me that more than half of the girls who worked there (a total of about 30) were "bonded girls" in the same way that Lek was. The amount the agent paid the parents differed slightly, depending on the physical look and the age of the girl. He cited one case of a girl of 12 who came because her parents sold her for 500 baht. She was too young to work, and was employed as an errand girl until she was old enough. The wife of the tailor who owned a shop opposite this massage parlour said that she had several times seen girls from the parlour with a bundle of clothes under their arms and tears in their eyes. Apparently an agent could get pretty rough on the girls when they refused to work. The receptionist said that they were not really beaten up, but they would not be allowed to go out of the building.

Had Lek had alternative employment in her village, her parents might not have encouraged her to have such a fate. It could also be argued that had Lek's parents had access to good credit or had the Government provided a better irrigation scheme for the farmers, the family would not have to live in abject poverty and drive their daughter to prostitution.

Pasuk Phongpaichit, From Peasant Girls to Bangkok Masseuses

Bangkok Restaurants

There are more than 50,000 eating establishments in Bangkok ranging from kerbside noodle stalls to international-class gourmet restaurants. This astounding figure (which leads to an equally amazing statistic: there is one restaurant or food stall for every 100 people in the city) reflects the importance Thais attach to food and the social act of eating. What's more, at even the humblest noodle cart one can expect to be served at least decent fare, if not truly glorious repast.

But not only great Thai food is to be had in Bangkok; excellent Chinese (especially Chiu Chow, Shanghai and Cantonese), Japanese, Indian and Middle Eastern foods are represented, as well as Western (particularly French, Italian and German) cuisine.

Below is a highly selective list of Bangkok restaurants. Adventurous gourmets will have no problem finding equally delicious alternatives.

Thai

Klang Soi
Soi 49, Sukhumvit Road
tel. 391-4988
11 am–9 pm
Set in a wooden house, this informal restaurant features very good Thai home cooking from all regions. Good prices.

Bussaracum
35 Soi Pipat 1 (off Convent Road)
tel. 235-8915
Open 4-10.30 pm daily

Piman Thai Theater Restaurant
46 Soi 49 Sukhumvit Road
tel. 258-7866
Open 7–9 pm. Reservations required.
Features Thai classical dance and music.

The Lemongrass Restaurant
5/1 Sukhumvit Soi 24
tel. 258-8637
Open 11 am–2 pm, 6–11 pm
Delicious Thai nouvelle cuisine in a very elegant setting but with reasonable prices.

Krua Taow Garden Restaurant
32/1, Soi 39, Sukhumvit Road
tel. 258-8273
Open 4–11 pm
Garden or air-conditioned seating areas.

Saem San Restaurant
65 Sukhumvit Soi 31
tel. 258-4582
Open 11 am–2 pm, 5–11 pm
Oysters on the half-shell and grilled Thai style steak are specialities here.

D'Jit Pochana II
Across the river from the Oriental Hotel in Thonburi. Lovely riverside setting.

The Seafood Market
388 Sukhumvit Road
tel. 258-0218/9
Open 9 am–midnight daily

Ban Chiang
14 Srivieng Road (next to Silom Club)
tel. 236-7045
Open 10.30 am–2.30 pm, 4.30–10.30 pm

Tum Nak Thai Garden Restaurant
131 Ratchadapisek Road
tel. 277-8833, 276-1810/2
Open daily 11 am–midnight.
Seating 3,000 people and covering four hectares (ten acres). One of the world's largest restaurants. Good food served by waiters on roller skates!

American and Steaks

The Angus Steak House
9/4-5 Thaniya Road
tel. 234-3590
Open 11.30 am–11 pm

Neil's Tavern
58/4 Soi Ruamrudi (Off Wireless Road)
tel. 251-5644
Open 11 am–2 pm, 6–11 pm

Gourmet Gallery
6/1 Soi Promsri 1, Sukhumvit Road
tel. 391-4811, 381-1270
Open 10 am–10 pm
Modern art and classical music compliment
this quiet candle-lit restaurant.

Chinese

New Great Shanghai Restaurant
648-52 Sukhumvit Road
tel. 258-7042, 258-8746
Open 11 am–11 pm

The Golden Dragon
108-14 Sukhumvit Road (near Soi 4)
tel. 251-4553, 252-7412
Open 11 am–2 pm, 6–10 pm

English

Bobby's Arms Pub and Restaurant
Patpong 2 Road Carpark Building
tel. 233-6828, 234-5987
Great fish and chips.

French

Le Bistrot
20/18-19 Ruamrudee Village
Soi Ruamrudee
tel. 251-2523
Open 11.30 am–2.30 pm, 6.30–11.30 pm

Le Banyan
59, Soi 8, Sukhumvit Road
tel. 253-5556, 253-4560
Open 12–2pm, 7-10 pm. Closed Sunday.
Expensive but very good.

German

Bei Otto
1, Soi 20, Sukhumvit Road
tel. 258-1496
8 am–1 am
Good German food.

Indian

Himali-Cha Cha
1229 New Road (near the corner of Surawong
Road)
tel. 235-1569
Open 11 am–11 pm
Fabulous chicken curries.

Italian

L'Opera
55 Soi 39 Sukhumvit Road
tel. 258-5605
Open daily 11.30 am–2 pm, 6–11 pm
Fine Italian food.

Japanese

Shin Daikoku
Off Asoke Road
Sukhumvit
tel. 254-9980/4
Traditional Japanese fare.

Korean

New Korea Restaurant
41/1 Sukhumvit Soi 19
tel. 253-5273
Open 10 am–2 pm, 5–10 pm

Lebanese

The Cedars
4/1, Soi 49/9 Sukhumvit Road
tel. 392-0292
Very generous helpings.

Norden

Norden Restaurant
1 Soi 20 Sukhumvit
tel. 258-1496
Open daily 11 am–11 pm
Smorgasbord Sundays noon-5 pm

Swiss

Fondue House
31/1 Wireless Road
tel. 253-7959
Open daily 11.30 am–2 pm, 6–11 pm
Features cheese and beef fondues.

Vegetarian

The Whole Earth Restaurant
93/3 Soi Langsuan
tel. 252-5574
Open 4 pm–midnight
Meat dishes also served

Vietnamese

Le Dalat
47/1 Soi 23, Sukhumvit Road
tel. 258-4192, 260-1849
Open 11.30 am–2.30 pm, 6–10 pm
Excellent Vietnamese cuisine served in an
elegant home setting.

Train Schedules and Fares

All trains run daily unless otherwise stated.

Advance booking Tickets of all classes may be purchased 30 days in advance at principal stations during the time advertised at each station and at the Advance Booking Office (in Bangkok Station) where the tickets to and from any station by all trains are obtainable 8.30 am−6 pm on weekdays and 8.30 am−noon on Saturdays, Sundays and official holidays.

Reservations from abroad may be made by mail, enclosing a bank draft to cover the amount of fares and charges and allowing ample time for a reply. Telex: 7242 SRTBKK TH.

Tickets are valid on the date and train as specified on the tickets only.

Change of journeys Passengers may change their journey to a later or earlier train or date. This is allowed twice but in case of postponement the total number of days must not exceed seven. Fee of ฿2, 5, 10, 20 or 40 is payable if ticket is reserved or unreserved.

Refund on tickets Passengers may apply for refund of the cost of tickets they are unable to use to the station-master at the station where the tickets were obtained not later than three hours after the departure time of the train by which they intended to travel. Refund fees vary from ten to 40 percent of ticket value but are not more than ฿300, for through-ticket to Malaysia and Singapore not more than ฿320 (per ticket). Fees vary according to the time of notification.

Children's fare Children three to 12 years old whose height does not exceed 150 centimetres (4 feet, 11 inches) are accepted at half adult fares. Children three years or under who are less than 100 centimetres (3 feet 3 inches) in height arand abdicated in 1935, living in self-imposed exile in England until his conveyed free, providing separate seats are not required for them.

Break of journey Passengers holding tickets for distances of 200 kilometres (124 miles) (one way) and over are allowed to break their journey once at any intermediate station for a period of not more than two days reckoned from the day after the journey is broken. Tickets must be endorsed by the station-master and a fee of ฿1 paid at the station where they break their trip immediately upon arrival of the train. For a return ticket, a break of journey is allowed each way.

Supplementary charges All supplementary charges are good for one unbroken journey and with one passenger ticket only. When using another passenger ticket for the same journey, changing train or breaking journey, such charges are to be paid again.

Validity of return tickets All classes return on the same day for distances of one−100 kilometres (0.62−62 miles), three days for distances of 101−200 kilometres (63−124 miles), seven days for distances of 201−500 kilometres (125−310 miles), 20 days for distances of 501 kilometres (311 miles) and over.

Luggage allowance Passengers are allowed to carry personal luggage free of charge as follows: first class 50 kilograms (110 pounds), second class 40 kilograms (88 pounds), third class 30 kilograms (66 pounds). Children paying half fares are allowed half the weight allowed for adults according to class of ticket.

SOUTHERN LINES . . .

STATIONS		DRC. 171	EXP. DRC. 17	DRC. 233	RAP. 45	EXP. 19 SP.	EXP. 11 SP.	RAP. 43	RAP. 47	RAP. 41	EX 1
					🛏	🛏	🛏	🛏	🛏	🛏	🛏
		3	3	3	2·3	1·2·3	1·2	2·3	2·3	2·3	2·
Bangkok	d.		21.55	09.00	12.35	14.00	15.15	16.00	17.30	18.30	19.
Thon Buri	d.	08.00									
Nakhon Pathom	d.	09.18		10.29	13.59	15.19	16.31	17.18	18.49	19.47	20.
Kanchanaburi	d.	10.31									
River Khwae Bridge	d.	10.36									
Nam Tok	a.	12.20									
Ratchaburi	d.			11.30	14.43	16.08	17.23	18.13	19.36	20.35	21.
Petchaburi	d.			12.14	15.26	16.50	18.06	18.58	20.17	21.16	22.
Hua Hin	a.		00.55	13.10	16.17	17.38	18.54	19.49	21.05	22.08	22.
Prachuap Khiri Khan	d.		02.04		17.34	18.59		21.09	22.24	23.35	00.
Chumphon	a.		04.28		19.57	21.25	22.42	00.03	01.34	02.49	03.
Lang Suan	a.		05.25		21.18	01.29			03.00	04.07	
Surat Thani	a.		06.55		23.29	00.37	01.52	03.22	04.46	06.03	06.
	d.				23.32	00.40	01.55	03.25	04.56	06.13	06.
Thong Song Jn.	d.				01.35	02.43	03.59	05.36	07.18	08.34	08.
Trang	a.									10.10	
Nakhon Si Thammarat	a.								08.35		10
Phatthalung	d.				03.15	04.26	05.41	07.15			
Hat Yai Jn.	a.				04.32	05.47	07.04	08.50			
	d.				04.52	06.05	07.19	09.15			
Yala	a.				06.34	07.43		11.00			
Sungai Kolok	a.				08.35	09.45					
Padang Besar	a.						08.00				
	d.						09.00				
Butterworth (For Penang)	a.						12.25				

MALAYSIAN CONNECTION . . .

STATIONS		ER. 1 @	ER. 1 @	M. 51	B. 59	XSP. 3 A @	SM. 61 🛏	B. 53	SM. 55 🛏	XSP. 5 A @	M 5
		2.3	2.3	2.3	2.3	1.2	1.2	2.3	1.2	1.2	2.
Butterworth	d.	07.45		08.30		14.15		20.30	22.00		
Bt. Mertajam	a.	07.59		08.47		14.29		20.48	22.17		
Ipoh.	a.	10.36		12.35		17.09		00.30	01.56		
Tapah Road	a.	11.29		13.52		17.52		02.09	03.24		
Kuala Lumpur	a.	13.45		17.50		20.15		05.30	06.40		
	d.		14.00		20.30		22.00			07.30	08
Seremban	a.		15.13		22.09		23.25			08.41	09
Segamat	a.		17.10		01.16		02.20			10.39	13
Johor Baharu	a.		19.49		04.57		06.00			13.23	17
Singapore	a.		20.30		06.15		06.55			14.05	18

BANGKOK — BUTTER WORTH

STATIONS	EXP. DRC. 18	DRC. 172	EXP. 16	RAP. 48	RAP. 42	RAP. 46	EXP. 20 SP.	EXP. 12 SP.	RAP. 44	DRC. 234
			🍽	🍽	🍽	🍽	🍽	🍽	🍽	
Class	3	3	2·3	2·3	2·3	2·3	1·2·3	1·2	2·3	3
terworth (For Penang) d.								13.40		
Jang Besar a.								16.05		
d.								15.55		
gai Kolok d.							10.05	10.55		
a d.							12.11	13.00	15.05	
Yai Jn. a.							14.00	14.40	16.38	16.50
d.							14.15	14.55	16.53	17.15
tthalung d.							15.34	16.17	18.14	18.49
hon Si Thammarat d.			15.30	13.40						
ng d.					14.00					
ng Song Jn. d.			16.43	15.02	15.47	17.17	18.04	19.58	20.30	
at Thani a.			18.44	17.25	18.10	19.18	20.09	21.58	22.43	
d.	11.00		18.52	17.35	18.20	19.23	20.12	22.01	22.46	
g Suan a.	12.28			19.21	20.10	21.22			00.55	
mphon a.	13.24		21.59	20.47	21.28	22.50	23.42	01.11	02.10	
chuap Khiri Khan d.	15.32		01.07	00.08	00.45	01.26	02.03		04.44	
a Hin d.	16.39		02.28	01.28	02.10	02.48	03.24	04.54	06.06	14.30
chaburi d.			03.21	02.19	03.01	03.41	04.17		07.04	15.27
chaburi d.			04.03	03.02	03.44	04.23	04.59	06.29	07.51	16.09
n Tok d.		12.35								
er Khwae Bridge d.		14.25								
chanaburi d.		14.30								
hon Pathom d.		15.58	04.53	03.54	04.33	05.10	05.49	07.19	08.45	17.19
n Buri a.		17.10		05.10						
gkok a.	20.00		06.10		05.50	06.35	07.05	08.35	10.00	18.50

BUTTERWORTH/KUALA LUMPUR/SINGAPORE

STATIONS	XSP. 2 A @	ER. 2 @	XSP. 6 A @	M. 58	B. 54	SM. 56 🍽	B. 60	SM. 62 🍽	XSP. 4 A @	M. 52
Class	2·3	2·3	1·2	2·3	2·3	1·2	2·3	1·2	1·2	2·3
japore d.	07.45		14.45	08.30			20.35	22.00		
or Baharu a.	08.13		15.13	09.03			21.37	22.33		
amat a.	10.56		18.05	12.48			00.54	02.13		
emban a.	12.59		20.05	16.01			04.24	05.26		
la Lumpur a.	14.30		21.25	17.50			06.15	07.00		
d.		15.00			20.30	22.00			07.30	08.00
ah Road a.		17.10			23.36	01.00			09.40	11.09
h a.		18.07			00.55	02.15			10.29	12.40
Mertajam a.		20.53			05.02	06.04			13.16	16.41
terworth a.		21.10			05.30	06.40			13.55	17.50

NORTHERN LINE ...

STATIONS		RAP. 59	ORD. 101	ORD. 91	RAP. 37 @	EXP. 7 @	EXP. 5 SP	57	RAP 35 @
		2·3	2·3	2·3	2·3	1·2·3	2·3	2·3	2·
Bangkok	d.	06.40	07.05	08.30	15.00	18.00	19.04	20.00	22.0
Don Muang	a.	07.21	07.48	09.15	15.40	18.40	20.20	20.40	22.4
Bang Pa-in	d.	II	08.27	09.55				II	II
Ayutthaya	d.	08.03	08.40	10.10	16.20	19.24	21.00	21.21	23.2
Ban Phachi	d.	08.23	09.01	10.38	16.41				23.4
Lop Buri	d.	09.03	09.57	11.33	17.28	20.24		22.22	00.2
Ban Takhli	d.	09.54	11.02	13.07	18.23				
Nakhon Sawan	d.	10.36	12.04	14.06	19.08	21.59	23.32	23.59	02.0
Taphan Hin	d.	11.37	13.36	15.52	20.13	22.57		01.23	03.1
Phichit	d.	11.59	14.09	16.24	20.37	23.20		01.50	03.4
Phitsanulok	a.	12.33	14.55	17.25	21.15	23.56		02.27	04.
	d.	12.35	14.58		21.17	23.58		02.33	04.
Uttaradit	d.	13.55	16.44		23.02	01.32		03.54	06.0
Sila At	d.	14.09	16.51		23.21	01.48	02.54	04.00	06.
Den Chai	a.	15.03	17.50		00.31	02.47	03.50	04.55	07.
	d.	15.06			00.34	02.52	03.35		07.
Mae Mo	d.	16.36				04.32			08.
Nakhon Lampang	d.	17.08			03.00	05.10	06.01		09.4
Khun Tan	d.	17.57			04.04	06.14	06.55		10.4
Lamphun	d.	18.51			04.51	07.01			11.3
Chiang Mai	a.	19.15			05.15	07.25	08.05		11.5

EASTERN LINE ...

STATIONS		DRC. 109	DRC. 151	DRC. 203	DRC. 183	MIX. 251	DRC. 187	DRC. 185	DR 18
		3	3	3	3	3	3	3	3
Bangkok	d.	06.00	07.00	08.05	09.40	11.25	13.10	15.10	17.
Makkasan	d.	06.12	07.19	08.17	09.53	11.46	13.21	15.21	17.
Hua Mak	d.	06.20	07.39	08.34	1012	12.03	13.35	15.35	17.
Hua Takhe	d.	06.59	08.04	08.59	1036	12.21	13.58	15.59	18.
Chachoengsao	a.	07.40	08.40	09.31	11.12	13.28	14.32	16.35	18.
Prachin Buri	a.	08.55		10.41	12.15	15.30	15.56	17.59	20.
Prachantakham	d.	09.15		10.00		15.58	16.17	18.16	
Kabin Buri	a.	09.45		11.30		16.35	16.45	18.45	
Aranyaprathet	a.	11.30				18.20			

BANGKOK — CHIANG MAI

STATIONS		RAP. 58	RAP. 38	EXP. 8 ©	EXP. 6 SP	RAP. 60	ORD. 92	ORD. 102	RAP. 36 ©
		2·3	2·3	2·3	2·3	1·2·3	2·3	2·3	2·3
Chiang Mai	d.		15.30	17.15	19.30	20.45			06.35
Lamphun	d.		15.53	17.38		21.09			07.04
Khun Tan	d.		16.42	18.33	20.46	22.03			08.05
Nakhon Lampang	d.		17.50	19.29	21.37	23.01			08.54
Mae Mo	d.		18.31	20.09					09.31
Den Chai	a.		20.07	21.43	23.47	01.12			11.03
	d.	19.00	20.11	21.48	23.51	01.15		06.00	11.06
Sila At	d.	20.03	21.17	22.54	01.04	02.31		07.26	12.10
Uttaradit	d.	20.10	21.25	23.01	‖	02.43		07.33	12.17
Phitsanulok	a.	21.40	22.53	00.13	‖	04.07		09.24	13.48
	d.	21.42	22.55	00.15	‖	04.09	06.05	09.27	13.50
Phichit	d.	22.24	23.37	00.55	‖	04.53	06.53	10.12	14.26
Taphan Hin	d.	22.56	00.02	‖	‖	05.18	07.26	10.50	14.50
Nakhon Sawan	d.	00.16	01.18	02.20	04.28	06.23	08.52	12.23	15.54
Ban Takhli	d.	‖	‖	‖	‖	07.04	10.10	13.23	‖
Lop Buri	d.	02.02	03.05	03.55	‖	07.57	11.34	14.34	17.29
Ban Phachi	d.	‖	03.48	‖	‖	08.46	12.36	15.48	18.20
Ayutthaya	d.	03.01	04.08	05.00	07.00	09.05	13.01	16.16	18.41
Bang Pa-in	d.	‖	‖	‖	‖	‖	13.28	16.29	‖
Don Muang	d.	03.41	04.48	05.43	07.41	09.43	14.07	17.07	19.23
Bangkok	a.	04.25	05.30	06.25	08.25	10.25	14.55	17.50	20.05

BANGKOK — ARANYAPRATHET

STATIONS		DRC. 182	MIX. 252	DRC. 186	DRC. 188	DRC. 154	DRC. 204	DRC. 184	DRC. 110
		3	3	3	3	3	3	3	3
Aranyaprathet	d.				06.40				13.05
Kabin Buri	d.		05.05	07.05	08.13		12.35		14.47
Prachantakham	d.		05.41	07.33	08.37		13.04		15.17
Prachin Buri	d.	05.20	06.08	07.50	08.58		13.22	14.15	15.38
Chachoengsao	d.	06.22	07.53	09.10	10.17	12.35	14.34	15.21	17.00
Hua Takhe	d.	06.58	09.01	09.50	10.57	13.11	15.08	16.01	17.37
Hua Mak	d.	07.24	09.32	10.11	11.25	13.36	15.36	16.26	18.10
Makkasan	d.	07.40	09.49	10.24	11.38	13.49	15.49	16.38	18.23
Bangkok	a.	07.55	10.10	10.35	11.50	14.00	16.00	16.50	18.35

NORTHEASTERN LINE...

STATIONS		ORD. 64	RAP. 52	RAP. 40	EXP. 2 🛏	ORD. 66	RAP. 32	ORD. 62	RAP. 30	EXP. 4 🛏	RAP 34
		2-3	2-3	2-3	1-2-3	2-3	2-3	2-3	2-3	1-2-3	2-3
Nong Khai	d.								17.40	19.00	07.4
Udon Thani	d.								18.41	19.55	08.3
Khon Kaen	d.								20.40	21.45	10.3
Ban Phai	d.								21.22	22.28	11.0
Bua Yai Jn.	d.								22.36	23.39	12.2
Ubon Ratchathani	d.	13.45	16.50	17.45	19.00	23.00	06.40	07.10			
Si Sa Ket	d.	14.53	17.49	18.55	20.07	00.11	07.55	08.29	*Via LamNarai Not operating on Nakhon Ratchasima Line*	*Via LamNarai Not operating on Nakhon Ratchasima Line*	*Nakhon Ratchasima Line*
Sikhoraphum	d.	16.19	18.53	20.04	21.10	01.21	09.09	09.49			
Surin	d.	17.02	19.27	20.47	21.46	01.59	09.41	10.29			
Buri Ram	d.	18.04	20.14	21.38	22.31	02.54	10.30	11.22			
Lam Plai Mat	d.	18.37	20.43	22.06	II	03.33	11.00	11.55			
Thanon Chira Jn.	d.	20.10	21.59	23.19	II	05.17	12.23	13.34			
Nakhon Ratchasima	d.	20.26	22.10	23.30	00.15	05.32	12.35	13.50			
Pak Chong	d.	22.25	23.47	01.06	01.49	07.32	13.57	15.34			
Muak Lek	d.	23.04	II	01.46	II	08.07	14.26	16.09			
Kaeng Khoi Jn.	d.	23.55	01.05	II	02.56	08.50	14.59	16.52	02.38	03.43	16.1
Saraburi	a.	00.10	01.19	02.30	03.09	09.13	15.13	17.05	02.52	03.56	16.2
Ban Phachi	a.	00.51	II	02.54	II	09.59	15.38	17.42	03.17	II	16.5
Ayutthaya	a.	01.18	02.04	03.15	03.56	10.25	15.59	18.04	03.39	04.40	17.1
Don Muang	a.	02.11	02.46	03.55	04.38	11.17	16.39	18.53	04.20	05.20	17.5
Bangkok	a.	03.00	03.30	04.35	05.20	12.00	17.25	19.40	05.00	06.00	18.4

STATIONS		RAP. 31	ORD. 61	ORD. 63	RAP. 39	EXP. 1 🛏	RAP. 51	ORD. 65	RAP. 33	RAP. 29	EXP 3 🛏
		2-3	2-3	2-3	2-3	1-2-3	2-3	2-3	2-3	2-3	1-2-
Bangkok	d.	06.50	07.15	15.25	18.45	21.00	22.45	23.25	06.15	19.00	20.3
Don Muang	d.	07.35	08.01	16.12	19.26	21.42	23.26	00.09	06.54	19.42	21.1
Ayutthaya	d.	08.14	08.58	16.59	20.07	22.24	00.08	00.56	07.32	20.23	21.5
Ban Phachi	d.	08.35	09.23	17.24	20.29	II	II	01.19	07.52	II	II
Saraburi	d.	08.57	10.13	17.58	20.52	23.06	00.48	01.54	08.14	21.01	22.3
Kaeng Khoi Jn.	d.	09.10	10.29	18.19	II	23.25	01.03	02.21	08.27	21.15	22.5
Muak Lek	d.	09.44	11.14	19.02	II	II	01.45	03.31	*Via LamNarai Not operating on Nakhon Ratchasima Line*	*Via LamNarai Not operating on Nakhon Ratchasima Line*	*Nakhon Ratchasima Line*
Pak Chong	d.	10.17	11.55	19.40	22.24	00.38	02.36	04.08			
Nakhon Ratchasima	d.	11.36	13.58	21.28	23.56	01.58	04.02	05.35			
Thanon Chira Jn.	d.	11.44	14.04	21.35	00.08	II	04.09	05.41			
Lam Phai Mat	d.	12.53	15.28	23.41	01.15	II	05.23	07.18			
Buri Ram	a.	13.17	16.01	00.12	01.46	03.35	05.52	07.55			
Surin	a.	14.05	16.57	01.07	02.36	04.20	06.42	08.55			
Sikhoraphum	a.	14.36	17.43	02.00	03.11	04.57	07.16	09.46			
Si Sa Ket	a.	15.40	19.21	03.13	04.16	05.57	08.26	11.03			
Ubon Ratchathani	a.	16.45	20.35	04.20	05.20	07.05	09.35	12.20			
Bua Yai Jn.	a.								12.19	01.21	02.5
Ban Phai	a.								13.29	02.35	04.0
Khon Kaen	a.								14.06	03.16	04.4
Udon Thani	a.								15.56	05.15	06.3
Nong Khai	a.								16.50	06.15	07.3

TRAIN FARES

SOUTHERN LINE AND WESTERN LINE

FROM BANGKOK TO		SINGLE		
Stations	kms.	1st	2nd	3rd
Nakhon Pathom	64	54	28	14
Kanchanaburi	133	111	57	28
River Khwae Bridge	136	115	59	29
Nam Tok	210	168	85	41
Ratchaburi	117	99	52	25
Phetchabrui	167	138	71	34
Hua Hin	229	182	92	44
Prachuap Khiri Khan	318	245	122	58
Chumphon	485	356	172	82
Surat Thani	651	470	224	107
Thung Song	773	550	261	124
Trang	845	597	282	135
Nakhon Si Thammarat	832	590	279	133
Phatthalung	862	611	288	137
Hat Yai	945	664	313	149
Yala	1,055	738	346	165
Sungai Kolok	1,159	808	378	180
Padang Besar	990	694	326	156
Butterworth	1,149	927	431	
Kuala Lumpur	1,531	1,432	659	
Singapore	1,927	1,965	899	

NORTHERN LINE

FROM BANGKOK TO		SINGLE		
Stations	kms.	1st	2nd	3rd
Don Muang	22	18	10	5
Bang Pa-in	58	49	26	12
Ayutthaya	71	60	31	15
Lop Buri	133	111	57	28
Ban Takhli	193	157	80	39
Nakhon Sawan	246	197	99	48
Taphan Hin	319	245	122	58
Phichit	347	266	131	63
Phitsanulok	389	292	143	69
Uttaradit	485	356	172	82
Sila At	488	359	174	83
Den Chai	534	389	188	90
Mae Mo	609	440	211	100
Nakhon Lampang	642	463	221	106
Khun Tan	683	490	233	111
Lamphun	729	520	247	118
Chang Mai	751	537	255	121

NORTHEASTERN LINE

FROM BANGKOK TO		SINGLE		
Stations	kms.	1st	2nd	3rd
Muak Lek	152	126	65	31
Pak Chong	180	146	74	36
Nakhon Ratcnasima	264	207	104	50
Surin	420	312	153	73
Si Sa Ket	515	376	182	87
Ubon Ratchathani	575	416	200	95
Bua Yai	346	266	131	63
Ban Phai	408	306	150	71
Khon Kaen	450	333	162	77
Udon Thani	569	413	198	95
Nong Khai	624	450	215	103

SUPPLEMENTARY CHARGES

Express train charge		Baht	30.00 per person.
Rapid train charge		Baht	20.00 per person.
Special express trin charge		Baht	50.00 per person.
Air-conditioned 2nd. 3rd coach charge		Baht	50.00 per person.
Sleeping berth charges			
Air-conditioned 1st class berth	double cabin	Baht	250.00 per person.
Air-conditioned 2nd class berth	upper	Baht	200.00 per person.
	lower		250.00 per person.
2nd class berth	upper	Baht	70.00 per person.
	lower		100.00 per person.
2nd class berth	upper	Baht	100.00 per person.
(Only special express)	lower		150.00 per person.
2nd class berth air-conditioned	upper		200.00 per person.
(Only special express)	lower	Baht	250.00 per person.

AIR FARES

SECTORS	FARE TYPE	FARES (BATH)	
		ONE WAY	ROUND TRIP
FROM BANGKOK TO			
Chiang Mai	Y	1,335	Double
Chiang Rai	Y	1,570	"
Mae Hong Son	Y	1,495	"
Lampang	Y	1,175	"
Surat Thani	Y	1,445	"
Koh Samuii	Y	1,780	"
Phuket	Y	1,620	"
Hat Yai	Y	1,850	"

Index of Places